# SEEDS

| Date Ordered | FROM WHOM | No. of Packets | Date Received | |
|---|---|---|---|---|
| May '30 | Germain's | | | |

# PLANTS & Bulbs

| Y | Date Ordered | FROM WHOM | No. of Plants | Date Received | Date and Place Planted | Date Bloom |
|---|---|---|---|---|---|---|
| ...ena | May '30 | Germain's (beautiful plants) | 2 | May | Lower garden "fen garden | |
| ...m | May | Jos. W Vestal | 2 | May | along wall | |
| ...a | | Marshall | 100 | | Nov. 14 upper garden | |
| ...low | | Marshall | 100 each | | Nov. 14 upper garden | |
| ...ies } ...ies } | | Max Schling | 12 24 | | nov. 7 upper garden outer row | |

# BAYOU BEND GARDENS

## *A Southern Oasis*

DAVID B. WARREN

Introduction by Mac Griswold

*Photographs by Rick Gardner, Don Glentzer, and Rob Muir*

SCALA PUBLISHERS

*in association with*

THE MUSEUM OF FINE ARTS, HOUSTON

SCALA

This book received generous funding from:
The Estate of Ruth Carter Slack in memory of her sister, Clare Carter Casperson
The Estate of Carol Clark Tatkon

First published in 2006 by
Scala Publishers Ltd.
Northburgh House
10 Northburgh Street
London ECIV OAT
www.scalapublishers.com

In association with The Museum of Fine Arts, Houston
P. O. Box 6826
Houston, Texas 77265-6826
www.mfah.org

ISBN 1 85759 423 1

Library of Congress Cataloguing-in-Publication Data available upon request

Edited by Christine Waller Manca
Designed by Bruce Campbell
Typography by Mary Gladue, Aardvark Type
Produced by Scala Publishers Ltd.
Printed and bound in Singapore

Jacket illustration: The Diana Garden at Bayou Bend.
Photograph by Rick Gardner.

# CONTENTS

# FOREWORD

The gardens at Bayou Bend are among the most beautiful public gardens in the United States. Originally conceived by the legendary Texas collector and philanthropist Miss Ima Hogg (1882–1975) to surround Bayou Bend, her magnificent home, the gardens are indeed an oasis of natural beauty and tranquility along Buffalo Bayou in Houston, the fourth-largest metropolitan center in the United States. In 1957, Miss Hogg made the extraordinary gift of her magnificent home, collection, and gardens to the Museum of Fine Arts, Houston. The house displays one of the nation's premier collections of American fine and decorative arts dating from 1620 to 1876. Both the house and the gardens are open to the public throughout the year.

Bayou Bend Collection and Gardens is justly renowned for its fourteen acres of exquisite gardens, as well as for its stellar collection of Americana. Nonetheless, this publication marks the first time that the gardens have been fully illustrated and detailed in a single volume. David B. Warren, the founding director emeritus of Bayou Bend Collection and Gardens, has brought a unique depth of knowledge to the subject of Bayou Bend Gardens. Mr. Warren retired as director in 2003 after a thirty-eight-year career at Bayou Bend. During his early years at Bayou Bend, he worked personally with Miss Hogg; more recently, he has conducted extensive research on the history of the design and execution of Bayou Bend

Gardens. This resulting volume captures the gardens' fascinating history and breathtaking beauty.

We are grateful to the estate of Ruth Carter Slack, a loyal friend of Bayou Bend; her bequest provided the initial support for this publication in memory of Mrs. Slack's sister, Clare Carter Casperson. A generous bequest from Carol Clark Tatkon, a supporter and past trustee of the Museum of Fine Arts, Houston, also helped bring to fruition this tribute to the beautiful gardens that Mrs. Tatkon so loved. We thank Scala Publishers for publishing this book in association with the Museum of Fine Arts, Houston.

In closing, we would like to acknowledge all those who have helped preserve and maintain Bayou Bend Gardens over the years. The wonderful gardens at Bayou Bend would not exist without the vision of Miss Ima Hogg and the participation of many others to help carry out and maintain that vision. A particular tribute is due to the River Oaks Garden Club. In 1961, Miss Hogg invited the River Oaks Garden Club to oversee Bayou Bend's gardens, and since that time, the organization's volunteers have devoted their time, talent, and resources to preserving and enhancing the gardens. Additionally, in 1967 the River Oaks Garden Club established the Bayou Bend Gardens Endowment Fund to safeguard the future of Bayou Bend Gardens. Over the years that initial fund has grown and its income has been vital to assuring the gardens' continued state of excellence.

Peter C. Marzio
*Director*
*The Museum of Fine Arts, Houston*

Bonnie Campbell
*Director*
*Bayou Bend Collection and Gardens*

# ACKNOWLEDGMENTS

This book grew out of an article commissioned in 1987 by Dr. Peter C. Marzio, director of the Museum of Fine Arts Houston, for *The Museum of Fine Arts, Houston, Bulletin*. Later, Diane P. Lovejoy, publications director at the MFAH, encouraged me to expand that article into a book. At the time this seemed like a rather simple idea. However, when I delved further into the project it became more complex as well as more exciting.

The *Bulletin* article had been based primarily on material found in the Bayou Bend files and in the MFAH Archives, as well as on interviews with C. C. "Pat" Fleming. For this book, a wealth of new material was found in the Ima Hogg and William C. Hogg Papers in the Center for American History, The University of Texas at Austin. In addition, I had the good fortune to meet and talk extensively with Albert Sheppard, partner in the firm of Fleming and Sheppard, which was so important to the final development of the garden in the late 1930s. These new sources proved invaluable in understanding exactly how the gardens evolved.

During the early stages of my research, Bayou Bend was fortunate to receive a generous bequest from the estate of Ruth Carter Slack in memory of her sister Clare Carter Casperson for a project associated with Bayou Bend Gardens. It was determined that this book provided a perfect fit with the bequest. Over the years, funds from that bequest were vital in supporting the research and assembling of material for the manuscript. More recently, a bequest from the estate of Carol Clark Tatkon was also earmarked for support of the book. I am exceedingly grateful to the executors of each estate for the two bequests that have proven so vital to the realization of the project.

The support of others has also been invaluable. I would particularly like to thank landscape historian Mac Griswold, who wrote the introduction to this book, as well as Judith Tankard, writer and historian, and Nancy Angell Streeter, the granddaughter of landscape architect Ellen Shipman. I am grateful to Pat Fleming and Albert Sheppard, who were there on the spot working with Miss Hogg, and Sadie Gwin Blackburn and Susan Booth Keeton, River Oaks Garden Club members deeply involved with Bayou Bend's gardens and supportive of my work. The master's theses of Kelly Allegrezza and Sally Banttari were each of great help; in addition, Ms. Banttari provided several key illustrations. Alice C. Simkins provided important access to the garden records of Dogwoods, Mike Hogg's home next door to Bayou Bend. Jane Karotkin provided photos of the Governor's Mansion.

At the Museum of Fine Arts, Houston, I would like to express thanks and appreciation to Peter C. Marzio, director; Gwendolyn H. Goffe, associate director, finance and administration; Margaret C. Skidmore, former associate director, development; Diane Lovejoy, publications director; Christine Waller Manca, assistant publications director, who has so ably edited this book; Lorraine Stuart, museum archivist; and Lisa M. Roth, who was my capable curatorial assistant. At Bayou Bend, I am grateful to Bonnie Campbell, director, and Bart Brechter, curator of the gardens.

I thank Bruce Campbell for creating the book's beautiful design and Scala Publishers for copublishing the book with the Museum of Fine Arts, Houston. I would like to acknowledge the photographers Rick Gardner, Don Glentzer, and Rob Muir, whose color photography captures the splendor of the gardens. Thanks go to Mary Gladue for typesetting, Anandaroop Roy for creating the maps, and Cynthia Bowman of Chas. P. Young Co. for providing prepress services.

Last, but definitely not least, I would like to express my heartfelt thanks to Ima Hogg. Her loving vision and guidance not only made the gardens at Bayou Bend, but also gave me inspiration to write about them, and left me with an enormous sense of awe at what she created.

*David B. Warren*

# INTRODUCTION

Ima Hogg. What *were* her parents thinking? As Ima herself told it, in 1882, her tin-ear father sentimentally called her "Ima" after a minor southern literary heroine. Hearing the news, her grandfather Stinson rushed to protest, but wasn't able to persuade his son-in-law to change his mind. The deed was done. The power of this unthinkable pun was so great it even engendered a mythical sister, "Ura," an invention of Hogg's political opponents. Ima transcended her name as well as all the jokes, however; she became a living Texas legend.

The name Bayou Bend, according to David Warren, also faced obstacles: Ima's elder brother, Will Hogg, said "Bayou Bend" sounded "muddy and muskeetery" to him. That's what "bayou" meant to a southerner in 1929. Ima stuck to her guns. Today the name means "Southern garden": camellias and azaleas, pink stucco and black ironwork.

David Warren skillfully disentangles the garden's creation, step by step, from some of its legends. He establishes Bayou Bend as part of the explosion of urban Houston in the first oil boom. He makes clear how precious the fourteen acres of gardens became over time. In 1957 Ima Hogg gave her house and property to the Museum of Fine Arts, Houston, and in 1961 she persuaded River Oaks Garden Club to take on the stewardship of the gardens. By making these donations, she gave more than architecture and Americana, flowers and trees; she gave the priceless gift of public space. She was also presenting her city with her own realized dreams.

The creation by a wealthy American woman of a complete domestic environment was not unusual in Ima's day. These places, often well-rooted in favorite versions of the past, were magic bubbles within which variations on architectural and landscape ideas could be played out as expressions of self.

How is creating place integral to creating self? Ima Hogg grew up in a military and political family which took part in the Civil War and the making of Texas. Her father was the first native-born governor of the state. "Home," for the four Hogg children, was more memory than reality. Ima grasped at the reality of details: irises later planted at Bayou Bend came from Mountain Home, the beloved Hogg plantation sold in Reconstruction days; roses and pink brick evoked her grandmother Stinson's vanished garden. For Ima, even the Governor's Mansion was more a state of mind than an actual place, since the house ceased to be "home" when the four years of Jim Hogg's tenure ended. Its memory is preserved in the curving stair and front hall at Bayou Bend. Three of the children, Will, Mike, and Ima, lived together for nearly twenty years, mostly in hotels and apartments. True "home" for them, and especially for Ima, was to be the place that she made. In 1925, brother Will wrote to her, "[It] is going to be your own layout, if you will take responsibility of dictating the whole thing."

Before that moment arrived however, in the fall of 1918, thirty-six-year-old Ima fell into the depression that would plague her, off and on, all her life. For two years, she was a "rest cure" patient of Dr. Francis X. Dercum, a pioneer neurologist, at the Jefferson Medical College outside Philadelphia. The patients who took the "rest cure," originally made fashionable in the 1860s by Dr. Weir Mitchell of Philadelphia, were almost all women. Many of them suffered from depression and neurasthenia, often brought on by the constricted position women found themselves in at the end of the nineteenth century: what roles would society allow them to play? It is no surprise that Ima, like other intelligent women, asked this question of herself and wanted help figuring it out. At one point, she had considered a career as a concert pianist. In some way, she was surely struggling to bring the claims of traditional femininity and those of the independent self into harmony. The biographer Jean Strouse, writing about Alice James, Henry and William James's sister, who was also

| VARIETY | Date Ordered | FROM WHOM | No. of Packets | Date Received | Date and Place Planted | Date of Blooming | COMMENTS |
|---|---|---|---|---|---|---|---|
| Lemon verbena | May '30 | Germain's | | | | | |

PLANTS & Bulbs

| VARIETY | Date Ordered | FROM WHOM | No. of Plants | Date Received | Date and Place Planted | Date of Blooming | COMMENTS |
|---|---|---|---|---|---|---|---|
| Lemon verbena | May '30 | Germain's (beautiful plants) | 2 | May | Lower garden upper garden | | one died for lack of water during summer |
| Rose Geranium | May | Jos. W Vestal | 2 | May | along wall | | Growing fine |
| Snow Flakes | | Marshall | 100 | | Nov. 14 upper garden | | Not very pretty |
| Freesias white & yellow | | Marshall | 100 each | | Nov. 14 upper garden | | Splendid |
| Calla Lilies Regal lilies | | Maas Schling | 12 24 | | nov. 7 upper garden outer row | | |

afflicted with acute depression, talks about the solitude of this condition, where a woman who could not or would not fulfill the imperatives of the day—marriage and children—nonetheless was unable consciously to reject them because she had internalized them.

Ima survived her treatment and conquered her depression sufficiently to live a spectacularly useful and fulfilling life. Her array of "good works" include her remarkable collection of American decorative arts, the founding of the Houston Symphony, and the establishment of a mental-health treatment center for disturbed children and their families. In Bayou Bend (and in these other works) she created a persona that was both a protection and a companion, as well as a fantastically useful apparatus that allowed her to participate in—even manage and direct—certain aspects of Houston's burgeoning cultural life. Within that carefully devised persona, Ima also found a freedom of will and movement that she otherwise might never have enjoyed at all.

Other resourceful American women escaped conventional expectations by the same route: Isabella Stewart Gardner (1840–1925), operating always at the outer limits of proper Boston society, devised a mirror image of herself in creating her "Venetian" museum, where her tall and eccentric (for Boston) building forms an elegant corset for the embellished garden at its heart. The strong-willed spinster Cornelia Horsford (1861–1944) used the 1735 house and garden she had inherited on Shelter Island, in New York, and its magnetic history of Quakers, Indians and slaves to set herself up as a colonial "Lord of the Manor." Lotusland, the exotic and wonderful garden of "Madame" Ganna Walska (1887–1984) in Santa Barbara, California, expresses the same prickly flamboyance in its world-class collection of cactus and succulents that "Madame" expressed in her life (six husbands, and a nearly lifelong quest to become an opera singer—a difficult task, as she had a terrible voice).

So part of the story of Bayou Bend is the often-told story of southern gardens: the transformation of Civil War trauma into romance. But Bayou Bend is also the story of "Missima," as she was often called. I end where I began, with delight in that amazing name: Ima Hogg was indeed someone who could make a silk purse out of a sow's ear. When a pool leaked, writes Warren, she transformed the leak into a cascade. When the Garden Club of America ladies arrived in 1939 for a "moonlight tea" to open the Diana Garden, a misty rain would not stop falling. Miss Ima just waited. One cannot force people to go outside. But a few eventually poked their heads out, and then more, and more. The garden, with its newfangled outdoor lighting and its arching jets of water that ardently framed—and still frame—the Diana statue, had become magical in the silvery rain. In the final analysis, you must work with what you have.

Mac Griswold

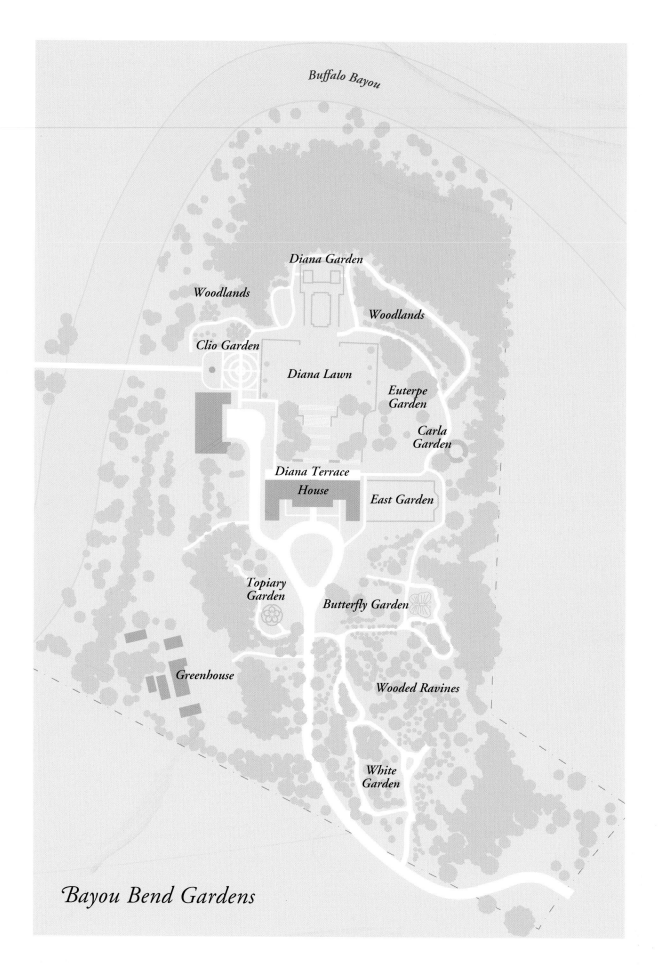

Buffalo Bayou

Diana Garden

Woodlands

Woodlands

Clio Garden

Diana Lawn

Euterpe
Garden

Carla
Garden

Diana Terrace

House

East Garden

Topiary
Garden

Butterfly Garden

Greenhouse

Wooded Ravines

White
Garden

Bayou Bend Gardens

# BAYOU BEND GARDENS

# A LOVE AFFAIR WITH NATURE
## MISS IMA HOGG'S GARDEN AT BAYOU BEND

*"Busy gardening and other things, we have squirrels, I just see one, and we have dogs but not many flowers."* [1]

These words, in a telegram sent by Miss Ima Hogg (1882–1975) to her brother William Clifford Hogg (1875–1930), represent the first, and not very promising, description of the garden surrounding her newly built residence in Houston, Texas, at a place they named Bayou Bend. Yet that garden, nurtured over the next decade by Bayou Bend's chatelaine, Ima Hogg, would evolve into one of America's great southern gardens developed in the period between the two world wars. Toward the end of her life, writing about her creation, she noted, "A love affair with nature is a rewarding experience. It gladdens the eye and replenishes the spirit." [2]

The story of Miss Hogg's garden is in a broad sense a reflection of national social movements during the period in which it was created. More specifically, the home and garden that would become Bayou Bend were shaped both by the evolution of Houston in the early twentieth century and by the Hogg family's participation in that evolution. Bayou Bend and its garden were inextricably tied to the development of the Houston neighborhood of River Oaks. Bayou Bend's creation and development were also heavily influenced by Miss Hogg's own past, her family's values, and her overriding desire to create something distinctly southern. While there were many people involved in the process, the southern garden developed by Ima Hogg at Bayou Bend was, ultimately, her own very personal expression.

### FORCES THAT SHAPED BAYOU BEND

Ima Hogg intended her new home and garden to embody all the graces of an antebellum southern plantation. The concept of "southernness" was one that was both explicit and implicit in the plans for Bayou Bend. Creation of the house and garden at Bayou Bend paralleled developments elsewhere in the South, where, in the early twentieth century, an improved economy led to new private fortunes. These newfound fortunes enabled southerners, for the first time since the Civil War, to build new and expensive homes surrounded by beautiful gardens. In the case of Houston and the Hogg family, the source of wealth was the emerging oil industry. Concurrently, the myth of the "Old South" became an underlying force in what is recognized today as a Southern Garden Renaissance.[3] Important Gulf Coast examples of this garden renaissance, in addition to Bayou Bend, include Shadows on the Teche in New Iberia, Louisiana, begun in 1922; Bellingrath Gardens in Mobile, Alabama, begun in 1927; and Longue Vue in New Orleans, begun in 1939. Like Bayou Bend, each of these gardens is notable for its collection of camellias and azaleas, both quintessentially southern antebellum garden flowering plants.

Another factor in the creation of Bayou Bend is today referred to as the Country House Movement, a phenomenon that swept upper-class America in the late nineteenth and early twentieth centuries. This trend began after the Civil War, when wealthy Americans sought to move away from the congestion and dirt of large cities and build homes in the clear air of bucolic, rural settings. The move away from the city centers was encouraged in part by the development of improved transportation—to a certain degree better roads, but more importantly improved and increased streetcar lines and railroads. In the initial stage, Americans looked to the landed estates of the English aristocracy as a model—large houses surrounded by vast acreage of farms and woodlands. George

Figure 1. The Governor's Mansion, Austin, 1870. *Courtesy the Friends of the Governor's Mansion, Austin.*

Vanderbilt's Biltmore (1895) in Asheville, North Carolina, is a prime example of this first phase. The second, quite distinct, stage of the Country House Movement witnessed the development of private residential enclaves at the edges of cities, often at the end of streetcar lines, and concurrently whole new suburbs, such as Philadelphia's Chestnut Hill or Chicago's Lake Forest, made accessible by commuter rail lines. In Houston, several enclaves were developed at the end of a streetcar line along Main Street; the largest and most important of these was Shadyside, the last such enclave developed before World War I. Ironically, had fate worked out differently, the Hoggs would have happily settled on a relatively small plot of land in Shadyside, and their ambitious home, Bayou Bend, with its surrounding fourteen acres of gardens, would never have been realized.

The third and final stage of the Country House Movement emerged after the turn of the twentieth century and the introduction of the automobile. This phase was characterized by extensively landscaped, planned garden communities, often surrounding a new country club, as seen in Baltimore's Roland Park and Kansas City's Country Club District. Both of these neighborhoods were models

for Houston's planned garden community, River Oaks. Indeed, the story of Bayou Bend is closely bound with that of River Oaks, which was developed by the Hogg family around the River Oaks Country Club. Bayou Bend itself was conceived as a crown jewel for that community, a paragon that would attract buyers to the Hogg real-estate venture.

Whereas the creation of Bayou Bend can be viewed as a part of broader American social movements—the Southern Garden Renaissance and the Country House Movement—the house and gardens are also a reflection of the Hogg family's personal experiences and aspirations. Several important factors shaped their approach. First was their family itself, from which they received a strong identity as heirs to a proud southern lineage marked by social and political prominence. Second was the desire for a new family seat to replace the one lost after the Civil War. The family's earlier experience in two other antebellum homes contributed to the concept—the 1857 Greek Revival style Governor's Mansion in Austin (figure 1), where the family lived from 1891 to 1895, and Varner, an 1830s Greek Revival style plantation house in West Columbia, Texas (figure 2), which their father, Governor James Stephen Hogg (1851–1906), purchased in 1901.

Ima Hogg and the two brothers who lived at Bayou Bend with her, William and Michael (1885–1941), were three of the four children born to Texas governor James Stephen Hogg and his wife, Sarah Stinson Hogg (1854–1895) (figure 3).[4] The Hoggs, typical of many early settlers of Texas, were descended from a genteel southern planter family that had, over successive generations, trekked westward in search of new and fertile plantation land. On the maternal side, their grandfather James A. Stinson (1829–1908), a colonel in the Confederate Army, moved from Troup County, Georgia, to settle in East Texas near Quitman after the Civil War.[5] The Hoggs, descended from Scotch-Irish stock who had come to Virginia in the mid-eighteenth century, moved progressively across the lower South. They followed a pattern of selling land at the crests of economic booms and using the profits to acquire more fertile land on the frontier, successively in Georgia, Alabama, Mississippi, and eventually the Republic of Texas. Joseph Lewis Hogg (1806–1862), the siblings' grandfather, settled near the East Texas town of Nacogdoches in

Figure 2. Varner Plantation, early twentieth century. *Ima Hogg Papers, Center for American History, The University of Texas at Austin (CN00997).*

Figure 3. The Hogg family, c. 1890. Left to right: Ima, William C., Thomas E., Governor James S., Michael, and Sarah Stinson Hogg. *Prints and Photographs Collection, Center for American History, The University of Texas at Austin (CN00347).*

Figure 4. Ima Hogg as a young girl. *Ima Hogg Papers, Center for American History, The University of Texas at Austin (CN11956).*

1836. A lawyer by training and a planter by vocation, Joseph Hogg entered the Congress of the Republic of Texas in 1844, and two years later he began army service in the Mexican War.[6]

Following the Mexican War, Joseph Hogg moved his family to land near Rusk, the newly established Cherokee County seat. There he built a new house and established a cotton plantation, which he called Mountain Home. James Stephen Hogg, known as Jim, the fifth child and third son of Joseph and his wife, Lucanda McMath Hogg (1815–1863), was born at Mountain Home in 1851. Over the next decade Joseph Hogg prospered. By the outbreak of the Civil War, Hogg was the owner of fifteen slaves and more than two thousand acres.

In 1861 Joseph Hogg entered the military service again, becoming a brigadier general in the Confederate forces. He lost his life the next year, dying of dysentery at Corinth, Mississippi. Lucanda died only a year later, leaving her six children, including the twelve-year-old Jim, orphans. In the economic struggle of the postwar Reconstruction era, the parentless family had little or no resources and became hopelessly burdened by increasing debt and escalating property taxes. By 1876, the original land of Mountain Home had been reduced to five hundred acres. At that point, with no means of raising cash to meet their obligations, the Hogg children were forced to sell their beloved family plantation. Jim, although not the eldest son, was asked by his siblings to arrange for the disposal of the property. The pain of losing the family plantation house and its land, that most essential southern possession, and Jim's family dream of its ultimate replacement remained at the heart of the Hogg family over two successive generations and impacted the conception of Bayou Bend half a century later.

Jim Hogg and Sallie Stinson were married in 1874, just two years prior to the loss of Mountain Home. Jim had little formal education but was eager to improve himself. He worked as a "printer's devil" or apprentice for a local newspaper, then studied law, and became a newspaper publisher and ultimately a newspaper owner, first in Longview and later in Quitman. Jim was attracted to the newspaper business because he saw it as a good springboard into politics, in which he soon became deeply involved. Having held several local offices, Jim was elected Attorney General of Texas in 1886, becoming at age thirty-five the youngest man to have held that position. That same year, Hogg moved his family to Austin, where they would reside until the turn of the twentieth century. In 1891 he became the first native Texan to hold the office of governor of Texas. He was governor for two successive two-year terms, until 1895. During that time, the family resided in the capital's 1857 Greek Revival Governor's Mansion. Although situated in an urban setting, the Governor's Mansion displays many elements of an antebellum Southern plantation house, with its towering Ionic-columned facade, wide central hall, and gracious curving staircase. The historic house and its antebellum furnishings made a deep and lasting impression on the young

Ima, as she later acknowledged, and strongly influenced how she conceived her dream house that would become Bayou Bend.

After Jim Hogg left the Governor's Mansion, he set up a law practice in Austin in partnership with Judge James Robertson.[7] It was around this time that Texas began to develop as a major center for the nascent oil industry. The law partners began to speculate in land, intending to drill for oil; in 1899, they bought the Gaines Plantation, an old property near West Columbia in southeast Texas. Two years later, Jim Hogg bought an adjacent property, thinking that it might not only have oil underneath it, but also that it might become a new family home. This property was what came in the family to be called Varner Plantation, named after the plantation's original land-grant owner, Matthew Varner. At virtually the same moment in 1901, Texas history and that of the Hoggs changed forever with the legendary oil strike at Spindletop, near Beaumont. Jim Hogg and James Swayne of Fort Worth joined forces as the Hogg-Swayne Syndicate and began dealing in oil leases in the Spindletop area. In 1902, Hogg joined together with two other oil business pioneers, Joseph S. Cullinan and Walter B. Sharp, to established the Texas Company (known after 1906 as Texaco). Although initially the home office was in Beaumont, the logical choice for the new company's base of operations would ultimately be Houston.[8]

Thus Miss Hogg's southern heritage was an influential factor in the creation of Bayou Bend, and a love of nature—trees, plants, and also gardens—was deeply rooted in her family background. Her maternal grandfather, James Stinson, was an avid horticulturist with extensive orchards and vegetable gardens. His wife, Mary, kept her brick-edged flower garden filled with spring bulbs and a great variety of roses; these same motifs appeared many years later in Miss Hogg's first garden at Bayou Bend. Late in life, reflecting on her abiding love of dogwood which were carefully planted in the woods at Bayou Bend, she noted that her only memory of the first few years of her life was an immense dogwood at her parents' home in Mineola.[9]

Sallie Stinson Hogg inherited her parents' enthusiasm for plants and flowers. This she was able to indulge while the family was living in the Governor's Mansion, with flowers—coleus, begonias, geraniums—bedded out around

Figure 5. Ima Hogg (seated at right in the carriage) taking part in a flower parade, Austin, c. 1900. *Ima Hogg Papers, Center for American History, The University of Texas at Austin (CN11958).*

From an early age, like her parents and grandparents, Ima (figure 4) was a lover of flowers. In 1894, at the age of twelve, she accompanied her father, by then a leading national figure in the Democratic Party, on a political trip to the East. Sallie stayed in Austin, but the young Ima's letters home share her travel experiences with her mother. Her observations vary from fascination with a player piano to seeing "Sanders, the strongest man in the world." Yet she was not overly impressed with all the sights she saw; she found the streets of New York to be narrow and not nearly so grand as the wide avenues of Austin. However, what did impress her were the flowers in New York, which seemed both plentiful and cheap, although everything else in the city was expensive. She was excited by a visit to a New York flower shop, where flowers were stored in an enormous, room-sized refrigerator.[12]

In the late nineteenth and early twentieth centuries, many southern towns held festivals celebrating historical events or agricultural accomplishments. These celebrations often including flower parades, in which carriages, and later automobiles, were literally covered with a profusion of flowers. Socially prominent young ladies from the community and gentlemen escorts were selected to ride in the parade vehicles. Such parades occurred in both Houston and Austin, where one year, the young Ima was a participant (figure 5). By then a young woman, the girl who had written her mother about the flowers in New York was virtually floating in a mass of blossoms.

the house in the Victorian mode. In addition, she maintained a garden devoted to roses. Sallie kept the house filled with flowers, and every morning she put a flower in her husband's buttonhole; his favorite, his daughter fondly remembered, was "a small pomegranate flower."[10]

Jim Hogg, too, was interested in gardening, and while residing at the Governor's Mansion took great delight in experimenting with plants in his vegetable garden. At some point he had salvaged irises from Mountain Home, and those bulbs were transplanted to the mansion and to each of Jim Hogg's subsequent homes, including Varner Plantation in West Columbia. At Varner, Hogg planted large orchards and vegetable gardens and experimented with various types of new and improved plants.[11] Hogg's most enduring and most legendary legacy, in terms of gardening, was a request he left to his children upon his death in 1906. He asked that they plant two trees, a walnut and a pecan, at the foot and head of his grave in Austin's Oakwood Cemetery. He further asked that when the trees matured and bore fruit that the nuts be gathered and distributed to, as he described them, "the plain people of Texas" so that they could plant the nuts and make Texas a green place of trees. The love of trees and the preservation of existing trees would later be an important factor in how Ima Hogg would situate her house and lay out her garden at Bayou Bend a quarter of a century later.

## THE HOGGS IN HOUSTON: THE EARLY YEARS, 1900–1920

Their involvement in the oil industry made it almost inevitable that the Hogg family would take up residence in Houston in the early twentieth century. The city—founded less than seventy years earlier by Augustus Chapman Allen and John Kirby Allen, two brothers who were land speculators from New York—was named after Sam Houston, the hero of San Jacinto, that decisive battle where the Mexican army was soundly defeated in the Texas War of Independence. The town site, located sixty miles inland from the Gulf of Mexico port of Galveston, was laid out on the shores of the Buffalo Bayou, a tributary of Galveston Bay. Although Galveston had been the

Figure 6. Plan of residential enclaves in the vicinity of South Main Street, Rice University, and Hermann Park, Houston. *Map by Anandaroop Roy.*

to downtown Houston ◀

dominant city of the region throughout the nineteenth century, the advantage of Houston's inland location was made obvious by two major hurricanes—one in 1875 and the legendary storm of 1900, each of which devastated Galveston. The widespread damage from the 1900 storm and Houston's relative proximity to the burgeoning oilfields of East Texas were important factors for the selection of Houston over Galveston by Hogg and the other principals of the Texas Company as a base of operations.

The wealth of Houston prior to the turn of the twentieth century was based on cotton and timber. In the early 1900s, it became increasingly based on the new and fast-growing oil industry. Jim Hogg had thought that Varner, his 4,100-acre cotton plantation in West Columbia, some sixty miles south of Houston, would serve both as a home for him and his children and as a symbolic replacement for the long-lost Mountain Home. It soon became evi-

dent, however, that Varner was somewhat remote and not suitable as a place of full-time residence. Hogg took up living in a suite at the Rice Hotel in Houston, commuting by train to Varner on the weekends. In 1905 he was seriously injured in a train wreck, and he died the following year. Hogg's pattern of using some sort of rental situation as a primary residence was continued by his children for nearly two decades—not a situation conducive to creating a garden.

At the turn of the twentieth century, just as members of the Hogg family were putting down roots in Houston, the area of the city where the elite resided had begun to move southward, from the congested center of town to new, exclusive residential enclaves along South Main Street—Westmoreland, Courtlandt Place, and Montrose (figure 6)—following the pattern of the Country House Movement's second stage.[13] Access to these new enclaves was facilitated by the establishment of a new streetcar line that provided transportation to and from downtown offices and shops. The major impetus for the development along South Main Street in the early 1900s came from two philanthropic donations. The first was a large gift of land from George Hermann to the City of Houston. In response to this gift, the city began to develop plans for a public park in that area, ultimately to be named after the donor. The site of the new Hermann Park was opposite the second land gift which came posthumously from William Marsh Rice, whose estate had been left to found a new college, Rice Institute (later known as Rice University). The college, built on Rice's land, opened in 1912. Integral to the plan of the new campus, designed by the Boston architectural firm of Cram Goodhue and Ferguson and located on a flat, treeless site, was extensive landscaping and the introduction of live oak and cypress trees. This landscaping, with its large infusion of trees, was a totally new but very influential concept in Houston.

The year 1916 saw the inception of yet another exclusive enclave for Houston. This was Shadyside, a focal point of the Hogg family's residential plans for the next seven years. Joseph S. Cullinan, a founder with Jim Hogg of the Texas Company, and business partner of Will Hogg, retained the noted Kansas City landscape architect George Kessler to lay out his private residential enclave on thirty-six acres situated opposite Hermann Park and adjacent to Rice Institute.[14] Shadyside, developed during the years spanning World War I, was designed with two broad, boulevard-like streets and substantial, multi-acre lots. As with the Rice campus, a large number of live oaks were transplanted into the new development. The largest site was reserved by Cullinan for himself, where he built an important house that was intended both to impress and to serve as an attraction to prospective buyers in Shadyside. This strategy was used by the Hoggs a decade later when selecting the site and building Bayou Bend in their own enclave, Homewoods at River Oaks. That same year, 1916, Will Hogg took an option on the next largest Shadyside plot, Lot Q, prominently located at the head of one of the streets.[15] Clearly the Hoggs were thinking of establishing a permanent home there.[16] Indeed, had the proposed house in Shadyside materialized, Bayou Bend would never have been built.

However, by early 1917, with the world at war, Will Hogg recognized that a new house in Shadyside was some time off and entered an interim solution, signing a two-year lease on a house being built on speculation by former Texas governor Ross S. Sterling. The tile-roofed, stucco house was located at 4410 Rossmoyne Boulevard in the Montrose development, Houston's third residential enclave.[17] The Hogg siblings, Will, Ima, and Mike, settled in their new home in March 1917, living in a house rather than an apartment for the first time since moving from Austin at the turn of the century. Within a month of the move into the Rossmoyne Boulevard home, the United States declared war against Germany. Although the Hoggs had been in consultation with Saint Louis architect James P. Jamieson, the designer of Cullinan's own house, also called Shadyside, the momentous events of 1917 and 1918 delayed any real progress on planning a house for Lot Q in Shadyside.

Additionally, in the fall of 1918, Ima Hogg fell seriously ill with depression and the next spring was sent to Philadelphia for treatment.[18] By that time, Cullinan was finalizing the options that various buyers, including Will Hogg, had taken for lots in Shadyside. Will Hogg, totally preoccupied with his sister's illness and not feeling capable of taking action on his option at that time, asked Cullinan for a six-month extension. Cullinan felt that this would not be fair to other option holders and those on the waiting list, and declined to grant Hogg the extension.[19] This was a great blow to Will Hogg and a disappointment that started him on an independent course that eventually led to establishing his own private enclave, River Oaks, and building the development's crown jewel, Bayou Bend.

In early 1919, the lease on the Rossmoyne house having expired, Hogg purchased the property from Ross Sterling. The house, which was intended to be a temporary residence, had become a more permanent one, and in fact was home to the Hoggs for the next nine years. The next summer, they embarked on a program of improvements to the property, including plans for landscaping and a garden around the house. Although evidence about the new garden, undertaken with considerable input by Ima Hogg, is somewhat sketchy, correspondence between Will Hogg and Edward Teas, the proprietor of a nursery in Houston, gives some clues. The letters indicate that the plan included hedging on both sides of the lot, two lines of poplar trees planted on either side of the house, and shrubbery planted along the back line of the property with a banking of roses along the edge of the shrubbery. The shrubbery was to include a variety of colors chosen by Miss Hogg, although the specific plants are not noted. In addition there is mention of flowers, again without identification.[20] This information, while tantalizingly brief, represents important documentation that once she owned a home, even though she was away from Houston for medical treatment, it was meaningful for Ima Hogg to have a garden. Her deep concern for her garden, although professed from afar, became a recurring theme in the letters that she avidly wrote home in the summers after the garden at Bayou Bend was established. Interesting, too, in this first garden is the presence of roses, something that was a part of her past memories of the gardens of Grandmother Stinson and her own mother in Austin, and an element that

played an important role in her new garden at Bayou Bend eight years later.

## NEW WEALTH AND REAL ESTATE VENTURES, 1920–24

The early 1920s were marked by an energetic array of new projects for the Hogg family. Their activities were enhanced by a new income stream that resulted from the discovery of oil at Varner Plantation.[21] On the domestic side, plans for renovating the house at Varner, which had been devised before the war by Houston architect Birdsall Briscoe, were finally realized. The remodeling process radically changed the exterior appearance of the old plantation house (figures 2 and 7). The old two-story porch and balcony were replaced by a full-height portico with soaring square columns, not unlike the portico on the river

Figure 7. Varner Plantation, after its renovation in the early 1920s. *The Museum of Fine Arts, Houston, Archives.*

facade of Mount Vernon, and the roof was topped with a cupola, also like that at Mount Vernon.[22] At the same time, Ima began to embellish the grounds, adding a large planting of southern magnolias (*Magnolia grandiflora*) to the planting of satsuma and magnolia trees made several years earlier, prior to the house renovations. From these alterations emerged a romanticized version of an antebellum southern plantation home, overlaid with Colonial Revival overtones and equipped with modern conveniences, presaging what would be created at Bayou Bend. It was always clear, however, that Varner, often referred to within the family as "the country," was considered only a weekend and vacation house.

The lure of New York also attracted Will's attention, and in 1920 he purchased his first apartment there, located on West 44th Street. The following year, with guidance from his sister, he purchased a larger and more fashionable apartment at 290 Park Avenue.[23] Although both Will and Ima spent extended periods of time in New York in the next few years, Houston remained the Hoggs' home, and the concept of a house in Shadyside was not entirely abandoned. A flurry of telegrams during the summer of 1922 from Will (in Houston) to Ima (at the Park Avenue apartment) indicate a proposed trade of the apartment for Lot Q in Shadyside, now owned by William S. Farish, was being considered.[24] However, the trade was never consummated. Although the Hoggs were thinking of a new and larger family home, realization of that idea remained in the future.

On the business side, Will Hogg plunged into real estate, quickly becoming involved in two planned communities. Each of these projects had elements that would be developed and enhanced when the Hoggs undertook the development of River Oaks several years later.[25] At the same time the Hoggs consolidated their various business interests into a company called Hogg Brothers. Although the company bore a masculine name, Ima was always an equal partner. In 1921 the family began construction of a downtown office building located at the corner of Louisiana and Preston streets. Named the Armor Building after an auto agency that occupied the ground floor, the eight-story edifice was topped by offices for Hogg Brothers. These were comprised of a luxurious penthouse suite, a freestanding, oval solarium, and a rooftop garden.[26] The concept of an office surrounded by a lush rooftop lawn and garden, while unusual, was entirely in keeping with the familial sensibilities.

The crowning achievement of the Hogg Brothers real-estate ventures was the development of River Oaks and the creation of Memorial Park, across Buffalo Bayou from River Oaks. River Oaks had its inception in 1923, the year after the Hoggs' flirtation with William S. Farish's site in Shadyside. Two Shadyside residents, Farish and Kenneth Womack, along with Colonel Thomas Ball, began plans for a new exclusive residential enclave. Breaking with the linear development of the existing Houston enclaves southward along Main Street, this new project was to be located on one hundred eighty acres of somewhat remote farmland west of the city. The concept for the project reflected the third and final stage of the Country House Movement, in which a planned community was built surrounding a country club. The new development was to be called Country Club Estates and the new country club River Oaks. As with earlier exclusive enclaves, the plan called for a grand boulevard with a central esplanade, bisected by cross streets extending out for several blocks on either side. The boulevard, at first called Ball Boulevard, was later named River Oaks Boulevard; the cross streets were named after well-known country clubs across America, such as Chevy Chase and Del Monte. The new country club was sited at the head of the boulevard. Members of the River Oaks Country Club would be offered the option of purchasing sites in the new development. A young architect, John F. Staub, who had supervised work in Houston for New York architect Harry Lindeberg on the recently built homes of Farish and Womack, was commissioned to design the country club; Staub would become the architect of Bayou Bend.

Ball, Farish, and Womack were not the only ones making land investments west of Houston in 1923. Both Will and Mike Hogg were also actively in pursuit of open spaces there. Mike Hogg acquired a tract of 118 acres west of Country Club Estates. This tract, which he christened Tall Timbers, was intended by Mike to be used as the site for a hunting lodge and bachelor's retreat from city living. In November of the same year, through an entity named Varner Realty Company, Will Hogg purchased the 873-acre site of a decommissioned U. S. Army property, Camp

Figure 8. Plan of River Oaks and Memorial Park. Country Club Estates was the 1923 suburban development acquired in 1924 by Will Hogg; he added the Home-woods section and the tracts flanking Country Club Estates. Tall Timbers had been purchased by Mike Hogg as a personal country retreat. All these areas were combined together to create River Oaks. The large tract to the north was purchased by Will Hogg from the U.S. Army, then sold to the City of Houston to create Memorial Park. *Map by Anandaroop Roy.*

*to downtown Houston* ▶

Logan. That tract was located across the Buffalo Bayou from Country Club Estates. Although his original intention was to build yet another city suburb, Hogg realized that there was greater potential across the bayou in Country Club Estates. At the same time, with characteristic vision, he also recognized Houston's need for more park land. He therefore offered to sell the Camp Logan property to the City of Houston. His offer was accepted and the result became Houston's 1,503-acre Memorial Park, named in honor of those lost in the recent Great War.[27]

Even as Will Hogg was arranging for the turnover of the Camp Logan property to the City of Houston, he began discreetly to acquire acreage adjacent to Country Club Estates as well as unreserved lots within the development. With a major stake in the project, the Hoggs were able to buy out the original investors and gain complete control of Country Club Estates.[28] Mike Hogg agreed

that his 118-acre tract at Tall Timbers would be available for the extensive planned garden community that Will Hogg envisioned (figure 8). Projects such as Roland Park in Baltimore and Country Club District in Kansas City were models that he hoped to emulate. The renowned Kansas City landscape architecture firm Hare and Hare, hired in 1923 by the City of Houston Parks Department to succeed George Kessler, was retained by the Hoggs to create a master plan for the entire 1,100 acres of the new community.[29] Herbert Kipp, a civil engineer who had worked with Cullinan at Shadyside was also brought into the project, and ultimately it was Kipp's plan that was adopted. The final scheme included picturesque curving streets and open park spaces. In a break with the arrangement at the earlier enclaves, the lots of the Hoggs' project were not all similar, but varied in size from the modest to the grand. Thus, while the enclave still bore the mantle of

Figure 9. John F. Staub, architect. Model house for River Oaks, 1925. *Photograph by Hester + Hardaway.*

Figure 10. Herbert Kipp, engineer. Suggested sketch of "Contentment" (later Homewoods), 1925. *Ima Hogg Papers, Center for American History, The University of Texas at Austin (CN11959).*

exclusivity, there was also the opportunity for a range of owners from the wealthy to those of more modest means to live there. The Hoggs' own home site, eventually located in a separate sector of the development, would be at the higher end of the range.

While there were many attractive features about the Hogg project, there were also several negative aspects that needed to be overcome. First, the garden community and new country club were not only located way out in the country, in a direction that defied the prior trend for exclusive enclaves down Main Street, but also lay in the exact opposite direction from the Houston Country Club, which was favored by the city's old-guard establishment and was located east of the city, at Wayside Drive and Braes Bayou. More importantly, however, Country Club Estates was not directly accessible from downtown Houston; one had to drive several miles south on Main Street and then west a number of miles more on Westheimer

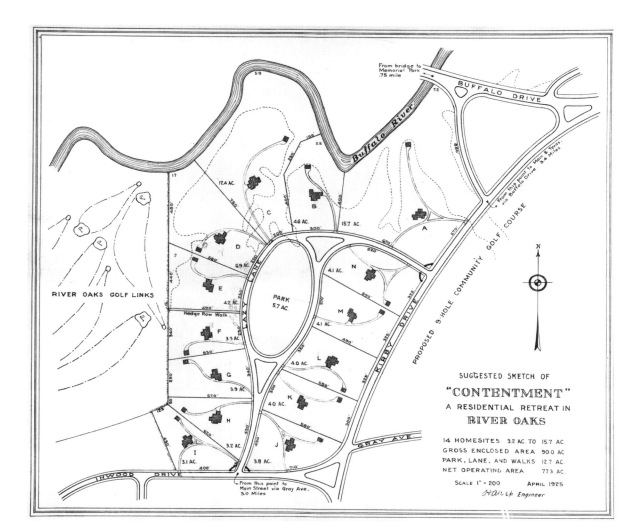

Road to reach the new River Oaks Boulevard. Recognizing this liability, Will Hogg arranged that part of the plan for Houston's new Memorial Park would include a road along Buffalo Bayou from downtown to the west past the edge of his development and then across the bayou and into the park.[30]

In addition to the clever marketing ploy of making the garden community more readily accessible from downtown, Hogg, through the managing company Country Club Estates, arranged for the construction of model houses designed by leading Houston architects.[31] One of those architects, John F. Staub, who had just designed the club house of the new River Oaks Country Club, was commissioned to design two model houses. The first of these, begun in 1924, became a collaborative effort between Ima Hogg and John Staub (figure 9). That house, completed the next year, had a noticeable New Orleans influence, and its pink stucco and black iron balcony from

New Orleans were elements that presaged what was developed by Staub and Miss Hogg at Bayou Bend several years later.[32]

## BAYOU BEND: A NEW HOME FOR MISS IMA HOGG, 1924–28

As the Hogg family, particularly Will but also Ima, was concentrating on developing their new real-estate project, it was inevitable that plans for a home for themselves would begin to evolve. Two plats for the River Oaks development from 1925 and 1926 (figures 10 and 11) show a ninety-acre tract, located east of the Country Club golf course, that was divided into fifteen individual lots, notable for their relatively large size.[33] Within the ninety-acre tract was to be a site for a new home for Miss Ima Hogg and her brothers, Will and Mike. Such a house would, as with the nine model homes, provide an important as well as prestigious draw to prospective purchasers of lots in Country Club Estates. Correspondence between Will and Ima indicates that the project for Homewoods, as the tract was named, would be the responsibility of Ima.[34]

Miss Ima Hogg's ninety-acre tract was intended to be an elite enclave within the larger entity of River Oaks, as Country Club Estates began to be called after 1927. The concept of large, exclusive lots was not dissimilar to that of Shadyside, although the total acreage of Homewoods was three times larger. Herbert Kipp laid out a picturesque, curving street, similar in design to that of Shadyside's Remington Lane but grander, with an oval, three-acre park in the middle flanked by small, triangular rose gardens at either end. The presence of the rose gardens reflects both the Hoggs' desire for beautification and their long-standing love of gardens, especially roses. The fifteen lots ranged in size from three to fourteen acres. Ima selected the largest, a site densely wooded with large old trees, located west of the main thoroughfare and nestled within a lazy bend of the Buffalo Bayou. She had been considering a name for the prospective home and, in the fall of 1925, discussed the idea with a friend, indicating that she wanted something that would suggest "quiet, contentment, country" and putting forward the name "Bayou Banks."[35] That name was adopted and used until early 1929, when it seems to have evolved to "Bayou

Figure 11. Herbert Kipp, engineer. Plat of "Homewoods," 1926. *Ima Hogg Papers, Center for American History, The University of Texas at Austin (CN11966).*

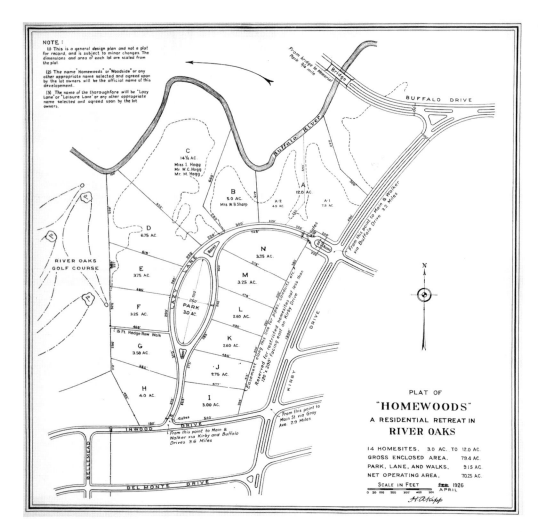

Bend." Although Ima liked the name, others were not as enthusiastic. Will Hogg wrote to her, "It sounds too muddy and 'muskeetery' and malarial to me. However . . . we will carry out your ideas." The evocation of southern landscape brought forward by the word bayou was significant to Ima, and she staunchly defended her choice of name in a letter to a friend in Massachusetts: "With a bayou running right through—and you know bayous are southern—and as everybody cannot have bayous, the idea appeals to me very strongly and . . . I am responsible for the name."[36] The curving thoroughfare of Homewoods was also given an evocative name, Lazy Lane—also suggesting quiet and country. Indeed, the building sites themselves were set back from the street and shielded from view by plantings in an arrangement that conveyed a rural feeling and provided a sense of privacy. This was in contrast to earlier Houston enclaves like Shadyside, where the houses with urban front lawns were clearly visible from the street.

By early 1926, plans for the new house and the grounds were moving apace. John Staub, Ima's collaborator on the River Oaks model house, and Birdsall Briscoe, an old family friend, were retained as associate architects. Briscoe, older than Staub, had worked with the family on the renovations at Varner Plantation several years prior and had been under consideration for the planned house on Lot Q in Shadyside.[37]

Working with John Staub on the 1924–25 River Oaks model home, Ima Hogg had contributed significantly to its ultimate southern character. Now, as Staub's client, she was even more deeply involved. The importance of southern architecture to her concept of the proposed house is evident in a series of revealing letters written in February 1926. In one she noted, "The house is going to be Southern colonial with a Latin flavor, if there is such a thing." A second letter relates, "The plan is at present to build hollow tile and stucco using very pale flesh color for the exterior and to use iron for the balconies and porches . . . I think the elevations are very stunning and [have] a great deal of the character of old Charleston southern houses, which has always been much my idea." In a third letter, she spoke about the collaboration of Staub and Briscoe, noting that occasionally it was difficult for them to accept her ideas; "however, I have gotten my way

about the kind of front hall I want."[38] In retrospect, it seems clear that the hall she envisioned was based on that in the Governor's Mansion; indeed, the hall there (figure 12), which extends through the house to a semicircular rear wall and has a curving staircase at the right with arched window above, is startlingly similar to the hall at Bayou Bend (figure 13).

A number of important precepts and thoughts that came together in the creation of the unique architectural design of Bayou Bend are in play in Ima Hogg's February 1926 letters. First is the concept of southernness for her house. In later years she recounted that indeed she wanted a gracious neo-Palladian five-part plan, but felt that a brick Georgian elevation, such as that of Carter's Grove in Virginia, Harwood House in Annapolis, or Homewood in Baltimore, was not appropriate for the Gulf Coast locale of Houston. In this she was very much in the mainstream of forward thinking. During the 1920s, leading American domestic architecture was strongly influenced by the Colonial Revival movement and by the idea that the colonial should be expressed in an architectural style appropriate to the particular region. For example, in Pennsylvania the prevailing style was the picturesque fieldstone house, which evoked an eighteenth-century farmhouse that had been added to over time. Similarly, Spanish colonial architecture was considered appropriate for places with warm climates, like California, Florida, and, to some, Texas. However, for Miss Hogg and John Staub, Spanish Colonial was not an option. Miss Hogg ruled out the style because it did not convey the antebellum southern character she sought; and Staub deemed it a style associated with places of arid climate, such as San Antonio, and thus not proper in the steamy, subtropical climate of the Gulf Coast. The dilemma, then, was to come up with something new, both southern and appropriate, but not derivative. As Ima Hogg had clearly indicated, the initial inspiration was Charleston, not New Orleans. Yet the influence of New Orleans cannot be denied, and the coining of the term "Latin" for their new hybrid style refers to the (non-Anglo) French and Spanish heritage of the Crescent City.[39]

What was beginning to crystallize in early 1926 was the concept of a romantic, southern plantation house, not unlike the recently improved Varner—yet better, because

Figure 14. John F. Staub, architect. Drawing of the south facade, Bayou Bend, 1927. *The Museum of Fine Arts, Houston, Archives.*

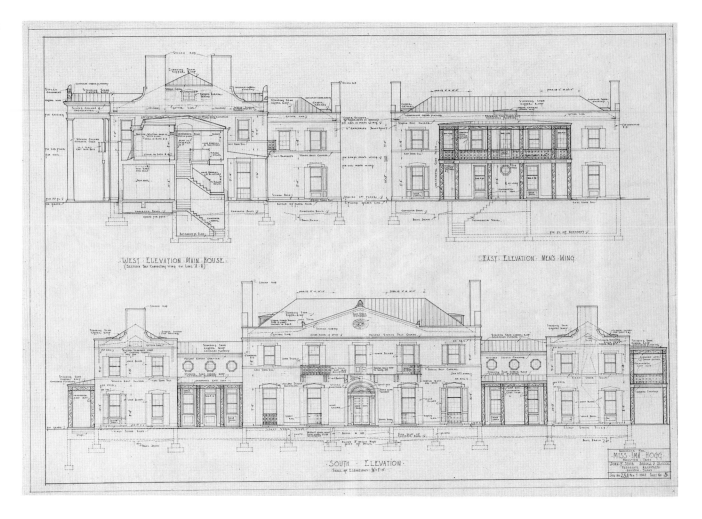

it was not remote, even though it was at the edge of Houston. Additionally, it would have a lovely, bucolic setting surrounded by the venerable old trees on the site, and an antebellum-style garden of southern plant material which would be developed concurrently. The new house would have all the conveniences of contemporary life—large closets, multiple bathrooms, and a modern kitchen. In sum, the concept of Bayou Bend represented something that for the Hogg family was ideal and that would at last replace Mountain Home.

By February 1927, Staub had made finished drawings of the elevations for "A Residence for Miss Ima Hogg" (figures 14 and 15). The design incorporated the antebellum-inspired pink stucco surface and black ornamental iron spoken of by Miss Hogg the previous year, but the clean, simplified lines of the elevations gave a modern look to the traditional, neo-Palladian plan. Acroteria, or decorative finials, in an anthemion design were placed at the peak and roof corners of both triangular pediments and

the oval sunburst on the south pediment; these provided visual references to earlier classical architecture and also to mid-nineteenth-century Greek Revival-style plantation houses, such as Belle Meade in Nashville, Tennessee (1853). More specific references are found in the design of the front door on the south facade, based on that of Charleston's Nathaniel Russell House (1803) and in the overall outline of the north facade, which echoes that of Homewood (1801), the Charles Carroll house in Baltimore. Interestingly, although those two houses, both made of brick, were considered valid design sources, their material was deemed inappropriate by both John Staub and Ima Hogg. That there is any connection between Bayou Bend's north facade and the design of Belle Meade, with its towering columns and stucco surfaces, had never been suggested, but there certainly is an analogy. Bayou Bend's black iron balcony, over the front door and extending across the span of the three second-story windows, is a motif also seen on the Nathaniel Russell House, and it was

*Opposite:* The south facade

Figure 15. John F. Staub, architect. Drawing of the north facade, Bayou Bend, 1927. *The Museum of Fine Arts, Houston, Archives.*

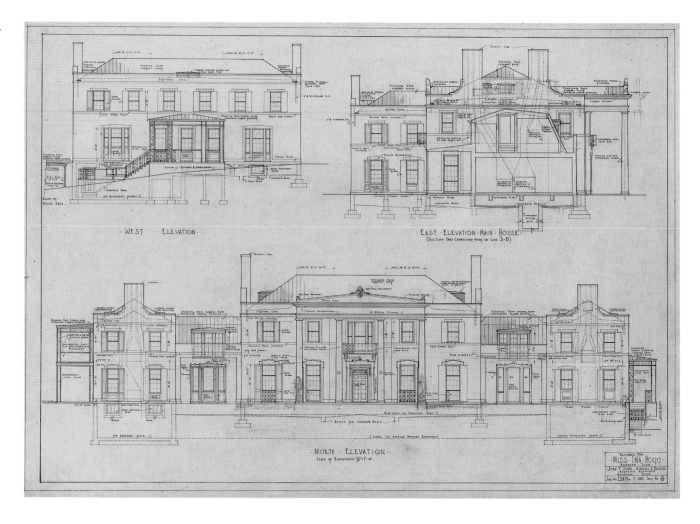

used by Staub on the pink stucco model house designed for the Country Club Estates in 1924.

The next month found the Hogg siblings intensely scrutinizing the proposed plans. In late 1926 the footprint of the house was staked out on the property and the siting was approved.[40] As with any building project, the clients found a number of things that they wished to change, and in this case the primary revision was the siting of the house itself. Will Hogg summarized their feelings in a strong letter to the architects: "It occurs to me that you had just as well set the house dead west as the way you have it. The house sets now as to catch the west sun on its supposed south front about 8 months of the year. We have got to live in the house always and comfort has evidently been sacrificed to perspective."[41] This exchange indicates that the house was originally intended to be oriented parallel to and overlooking Buffalo Bayou on the property's west side, much in the way that antebellum plantation houses were oriented to a river. As a result of Will Hogg's

observations, the house siting was ultimately turned ninety degrees to its final orientation—the north and south facades at right angles to the bayou. However, as the bayou course curved around the far north end of the property, the concept of a river side was not entirely lost. The revised siting placed a proposed porte cochère for the entrance facade in conflict with a large, old tree. In keeping with the Hogg family reverence for trees, the porte cochère was eliminated.[42] The same sensibility was observed when a pink flagstone terrace was built along the north facade of the house and openings in the pavement were made to accommodate several large trees.

Ima Hogg was deeply involved in every aspect of creating her new house. Throughout the spring and summer of 1927 she consulted with Staub about various details of the project, ranging from exterior ornamental ironwork to interior features such as millwork and paint. After they had traveled to New Orleans to look at both antique and new ornamental cast ironwork, they debated the issue of

combining New Orleans-style cast iron and Charleston-style wrought iron. While acknowledging that he thought Charleston wrought-iron balconies (like that on the Nathaniel Russell House) lovelier than those of New Orleans, Staub argued that a mix of media would not be as harmonious as if cast iron were used throughout. Staub's views eventually prevailed, and in the fall he placed a large order for New Orleans cast iron for use on the balustrades and porches of the house and garage building.[43] An antique balcony was purchased for the south facade. At the same time, Ima was in New England, independently seeking out eighteenth-century woodwork and other materials for incorporation into the interiors. Such use of period colonial architectural material for new interiors was an important characteristic of the Colonial Revival movement in America during the 1920s and paralleled the use of the antique iron balcony on the exterior of Bayou Bend.[44]

Construction of the new house began in 1927 and continued throughout much of 1928. Although the Hoggs, with their characteristic preference for privacy, had kept plans for the house quiet, the need to file for various permits let out sufficient information for a newspaper article

in early May 1927, which stated that they were planning a $250,000 mansion. On August 26, 1928, the *Houston Post-Dispatch* featured preview photographs of "Miss Ima Hogg's Home in River Oaks" (figure 16) and noted that the house cost in excess of $300,000.[45]

On November 5, 1928, the family moved into the completed house, an event succinctly noted by Will Hogg in his diary: ". . . home to Bayou Banks" and ". . . first night in Bayou Banks, today our first meal together."[46] The Hogg's new home embodied all the characteristic elements of an antebellum plantation. The pink stucco neo-Palladian-plan house was approached by a picturesque curving drive that proceeded about a quarter of a mile from the public street through towering pines, the vista opening up to reveal the first glimpse of the south facade (figure 17). As with many antebellum houses, the two facades at Bayou Bend are distinctly different from each other: the drive side with its attached triangular pediment and wrought iron balcony, and the garden side with its temple front of towering columns crowned by a pediment, facing the bayou at the north end of the property—in essence a land facade and a river facade, such as those found at Mount Vernon, itself the inspiration for the transformation of Varner Plantation a decade earlier. A more subtle difference is seen in the connecting elements, which on the south side are clearly two stories, but on the north side have the appearance of being one story—with the result that the central columned temple portico of the north facade is made to appear much taller. The concept of the two sides was played out in the initial placement of the gardens, in which the major garden, following antebellum precepts, was located on the water side, away from the main approach to the house on the land side.

## BAYOU BEND GARDENS: THE FIRST PHASE, 1926–30

At the same time that the concept of the Hogg's new home, a romanticized version of an antebellum plantation house, was beginning to crystallize in early 1926, plans for the grounds were being given the same degree of consideration. As with the house design, the concern to create a southern ambience was paramount. However, the family did not wait for the house to be finished, but rather

Figure 16. "First Pictures of Miss Ima Hogg's Home in River Oaks." *Houston Post-Dispatch,* August 26, 1928. *The Museum of Fine Arts, Houston, Archives.*

Figure 17. View of the south facade of Bayou Bend from the driveway, 1950. *The Museum of Fine Arts, Houston, Archives.*

thought about the grounds simultaneously, reflecting their equal importance. As the year opened, Will telegrammed his sister from Miami: "Missima having selected your home site have plenty magnolias yaupon, black and red haws holly persimmon wild peach crepe myrtle planted now in background and fringes." It is interesting to note the list includes a mix of southern native species, such as magnolia and yaupon, widely used in antebellum gardens, with crepe myrtle, an exotic, early-nineteenth-century import from Asia, that along with azaleas and camellias, also Asian imports, had become a staple of the antebellum garden. A month later, his sister indicated that she had acted on his suggestion and that the shrubs would be planted shortly. The idea of planting a profusion of dogwood in the swales and draws of the wooded sections of the property was adopted in April, and the two planting projects were accomplished by the end of the spring.[47] Once again, as at Varner Plantation ten years earlier, the family sensibility toward plants and trees was at play. Thus, even before work on the house had begun, the

Hogg siblings were giving careful consideration to the introduction of typical antebellum southern plant material onto the property. There was a strong desire to add a sense of historicity to the garden at Bayou Bend; toward that end, a huge, thirty-foot-high, sixty-year-old *Magnolia grandiflora* was purchased from an old garden downtown and transplanted to Bayou Bend in April 1926.[48] Concurrently, although his sister's new house was as yet unplanned and unsited, Will began to purchase a large number of pink flagstone sidewalk pavers from downtown Houston business owners who were, at that very moment, removing and discarding the stones, replacing them with modern cement. The idea was to use the pink stones as the surfaces for the terraces and outside walks around their new residence and into the woods. Incorporating the transplanted ancient magnolia and the old flagstones would lend a sense of age, history, and romanticism to their brand-new garden, echoing the use of antique ironwork and architectural details incorporated into the house.

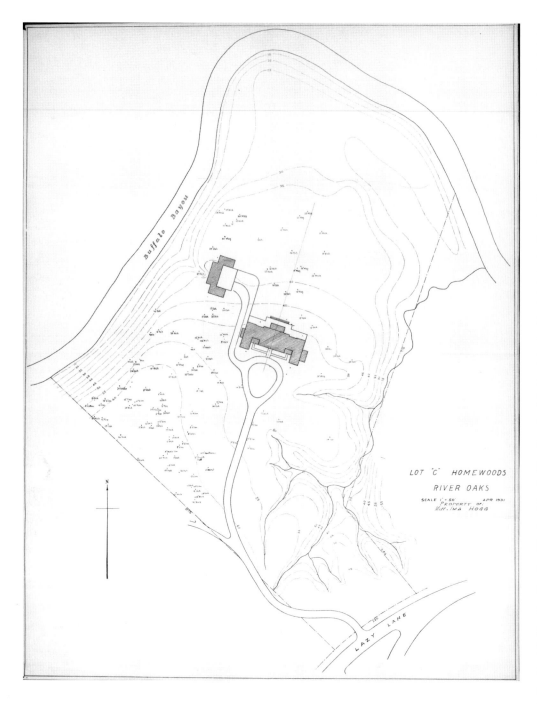

identified a total of 128 trees, including four different kinds of oak, elms, magnolias, hackberry, and paper birch, this last described as very rare.[49] The company was hired in December 1926 to commence a program of care for the trees. The Hoggs considered the woods surrounding their new home not only as a setting for the house, but also as part of the garden.

The area immediately surrounding the house itself was, naturally, of great importance as well. The earliest indication of what was under consideration is found in a February 1928 proposal (figure 19) drawn up by Hare and Hare, the Kansas City-based landscape architecture firm that had been consulting for several years with the City of Houston's Parks Department and that had initially been retained by Will Hogg to lay out River Oaks. Although their proposal, "Preliminary Study for the Property of Miss Ima Hogg and Mr. W. C. Hogg" was not implemented, it contained three important elements that would later appear in the garden at Bayou Bend. First, that there would be an interest in walking through the woods to the south of the house and that the area would be a part of the garden is indicated by a footpath leading in that direction, where today a path leads off the driveway into the woodland gardens. Second, the Hares' design for a garden extending from the east end of the house, with its lateral beds and exedra shape at the far end, presage what was developed the next year. Lastly, a significant element of the Hare and Hare plan is the terraced steps, on axis with the north facade, leading down the slope to a parterre garden and a tea house, which serves as a focal point, closing the composition at the edge of the woods. The clients evidently had their own ideas. Will Hogg had sketched out a related, unrealized scheme (figure 20) two years earlier.[50] The siblings must have discussed their ideas with the landscape architects, as witnessed by the woodland path to the south, and also the prominent notation in the rendering of the valued "existing trees," at that time under the care of Dr. Blume. Particularly noticeable are two trees that impinge on the western edge of the axial pathway leading from the house to the parterre garden, disrupting the symmetry that one would have expected there in that formal passage. The random quality of the existing trees in juxtaposition to a formal, symmetrical scheme is a detail that would ultimately appear as this area of the garden was

Figure 18. Herbert Kipp, engineer. Rendering of lot "C" of Homewoods, the site of Bayou Bend, 1926. *Ima Hogg Papers, Center for American History, The University of Texas at Austin (CN11967).*

Later in 1926, Herbert Kipp, the civil engineer for the River Oaks Corporation, as the managing company for the development was then known, prepared a topographical plan of the heavily wooded Bayou Bend site, including in the rendering an indication of the large trees (figure 18). With this information in hand, the builders retained Dr. Conway Blume, a tree surgeon and principal of a Houston landscape gardening company called the Blume System, to take an inventory of all the important hardwood trees on the property. Blume's report ultimately

*Opposite:* Aerial view of Bayou Bend

Figure 19. Hare and Hare, land-scape architects. Preliminary Study for the Property of Miss Ima Hogg and Mr. W. C. Hogg, River Oaks, 1928. *Ima Hogg Papers, Center for American History, The University of Texas at Austin (CN111965).*

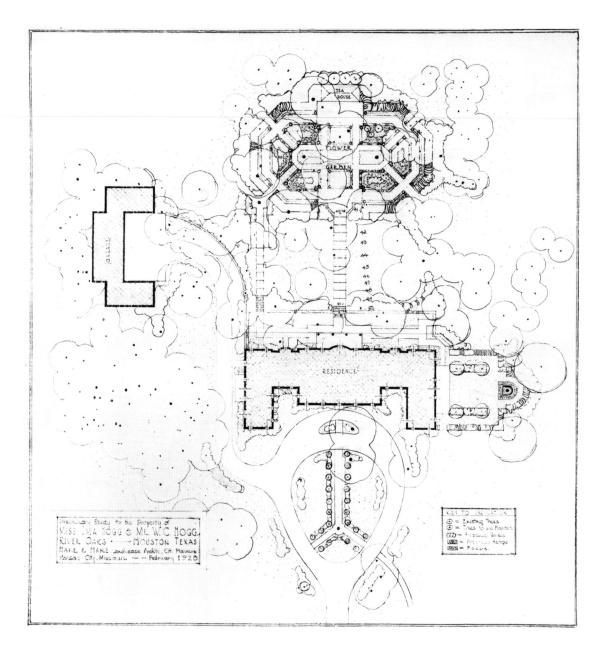

Figure 20. Will Hogg. Sketch of proposed "My Country Place." *Ima Hogg Papers, Center for American History, The University of Texas at Austin (CN111968).*

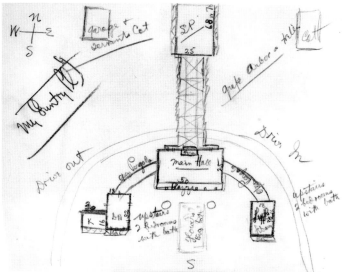

developed a decade later. Why the Hare and Hare plan was not realized is not clear. The drawing, apparently valued, was retained among papers pertaining to the gardens at Bayou Bend. There are, however, plausible answers. First and foremost, the plan was far too elaborate, structured, and formal for people concerned with the natural landscape and the picturesque, gnarled trees found there. Second, the plan would have been very expensive, and as with plans for the house, realities dictated that certain things needed to be cut back or simplified.[51]

Although there is no documentation of the progress in the gardens following the February Hare and Hare proposal, the August 1928 preview photograph in the *Houston*

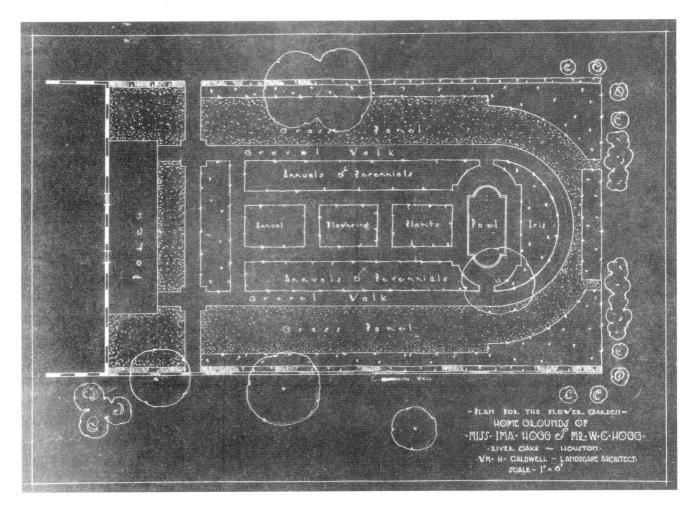

Figure 21. William Caldwell, landscape architect. Proposed Plan for the Flower Garden, Home Grounds of Miss Ima Hogg and Mr. W. C. Hogg, River Oaks, Houston, c. 1928. *Ima Hogg Papers, Center for American History, The University of Texas at Austin (CN111969).*

*Post-Dispatch* (see figure 16) reveals a sweeping slope of hillside extending down from the north facade of the house toward the bend of the bayou. That area, which had been cleared of underbrush, is punctuated with the large trees that were under the care of Dr. Blume. This slope obviously would become a broad expanse of lawn; an October 1928 commitment to install an extensive irrigation system just prior to the family's move into the house the following month indicates that a garden and a large amount of lawn surrounding the house were planned. That the garden at Bayou Bend was then somewhat incomplete is indicated by Miss Hogg's response to inquiries that fall that she was not yet ready to interview prospective gardeners.[52]

A simple ruled composition book used by Miss Ima Hogg as a garden notebook shows that by the fall of 1929 there were two gardens at Bayou Bend. These, then simply referred to as the upper and lower gardens, are known today respectively as the East Garden and the Clio Garden.[53] The upper garden, which was laid out at the east end of the house in the approximate location indicated by the Hare and Hare plan, was created first. Clues to who designed the garden and the approximate date of layout are found in the final accounting for the expenses of building Bayou Bend. Included is the sizeable payment of $1,998 to the "Houston Landscaping Company." The 1928 Houston City Directory lists the firm and its president, William H. Caldwell. A drawing titled "Plan for the Flower Garden—Home Grounds of Miss Ima Hogg and Mr. W. C. Hogg" and signed "Wm. H. Caldwell, Landscape Architect" (figure 21) provides an important documentary link.[54] The drawing, which shows a large porch at the left, surely depicts the site of today's East Porch and East Garden. Caldwell's exedra-shaped end and lateral beds, which likely are derived from the Hare and Hare scheme, also appear in Miss Hogg's notebook drawing of the upper garden made in the fall of 1929 (figure 22). No further payments were made to Houston Landscaping

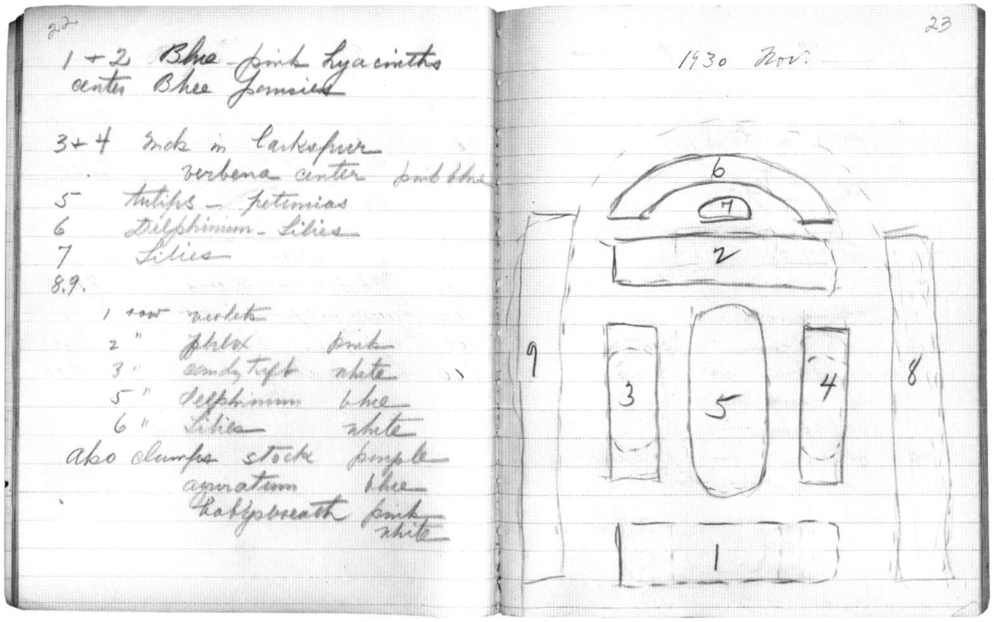

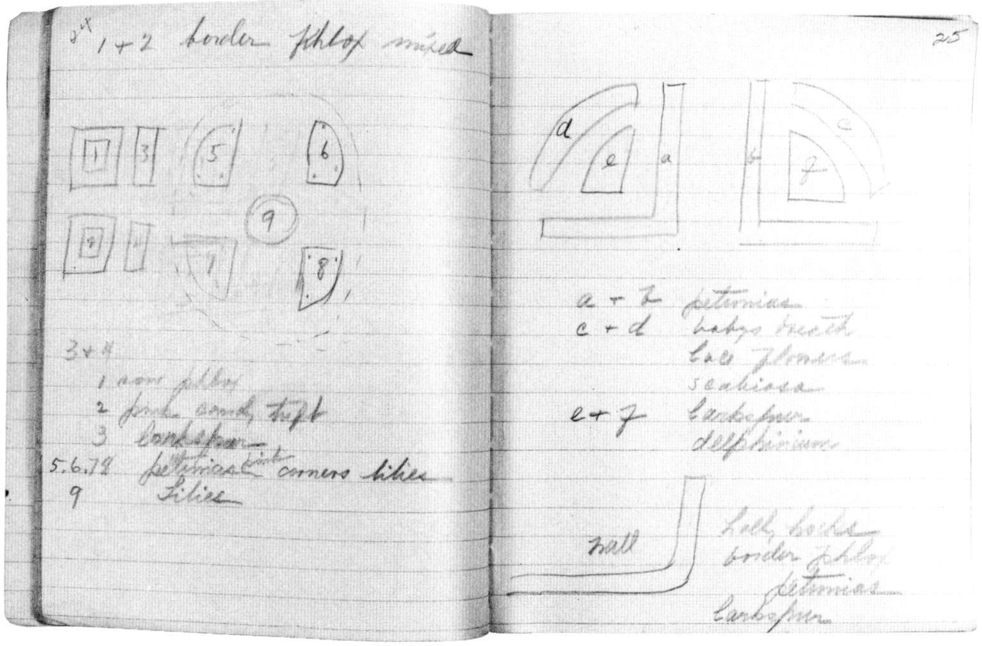

Figure 22. Sketch of the Upper Garden (now the East Garden) in Ima Hogg's garden notebook, 1929. *The Museum of Fine Arts, Houston, Archives.*

Figure 23. Sketch of the Lower Garden (now the Clio Garden) in Ima Hogg's garden notebook, 1929. *The Museum of Fine Arts, Houston, Archives.*

Company after October 1928, indicating that they had already rendered their services by that time and suggesting that the upper garden had been laid out when the Hoggs moved into the house. The Caldwell plan called for grass panels and gravel walks with beds of annuals, perennials, and irises massed at the east end, just beyond a formal rectangular pool with semicircular ends.[55] The actual garden as drawn by Miss Hogg for her garden notebook features annuals, perennials, and bulbs bedded out in the lawn—not unlike Caldwell's proposal, but the overall design is far less structured than the Caldwell drawing and shows that the formal element of a pool at the east end was not included. This virtual lack of structure and overall informality are very much in keeping with Miss Hogg's sensibility for simplicity and naturalness. The numbered guide on the page next to the garden sketch lists the various plants for each bed. Included are a mix of early blooming varieties, like pansies, hyacinths, and tulips, and late spring–early summer flowers—violets, larkspur, verbena, delphinium, phlox, candy tuft, stock, ageratum, baby's breath, and white lilies. The color palette is—with the exception of the purple stock—blue, white, and pink. These last two colors were particular favorites of Miss Hogg, and she brought them into her garden with various plants throughout her gardening career.

The second garden, also documented in Miss Hogg's notebook (figure 23), was located to the north of the house, down at the bottom of the hill between the western edge of the sloping lawn and the bayou, adjacent to the "Gardener's Cottage." The formal design features walks and beds in concentric circles around a central, circular bed, with cross walks at right angles—all contained within a square—and a D-shaped area to the west of the square. Although the formality of the design might at first seem incongruous with Miss Hogg's sensibilities, what is reflected there is the tradition of antebellum plantation gardens, which commonly featured highly structured, geometric design.[56] As with typical antebellum ornamental gardens, this one at Bayou Bend is placed on the "water" side of the house. Miss Hogg acted on the desire to evoke the antebellum era in a very personal way by situating her formal, structured garden neither on axis with nor highly visible from the house, as is customary with antebellum precedents, but set to the left or west, out of view of the house. Similarly the upper, east garden was set to the right, also out of the main line of view. In this manner, Miss Hogg was able to maintain the uninterrupted sweep of naturalistic sloping lawn punctuated with the gnarled old trees as the major visual focus when the garden was viewed from the house.

William Caldwell probably made the plan for the lower, parterre garden, although no documentation of his participation survives. The walks of the garden are paved and the beds edged with old, pale pink brick, which was purchased in April 1929, thus establishing spring and early summer as the time of the garden's construction.[57] The use of antique brick, which parallels the earlier use of the old pink flagstone around the house, again provides a romantic sense of age for the newly created garden. The brick-edged beds also recall those remembered by Miss Hogg in her Grandmother Stinson's rose garden, which well may have been the inspiration for this neo-antebellum garden at Bayou Bend. While Miss Hogg's sketch of the garden's plant material shows that it was very similar to that of the upper garden, there are indications that this was to become a rose garden. Indeed, as this garden was being built, advertisements searching for gardeners, placed by the Hoggs in local papers during April 1929, specified that candidates must have knowledge of how to care for roses. By May, a garden staff of three was in place and the gardens at Bayou Bend began their first full season.[58] The gardens must have been relatively complete by that time, as Will Hogg noted in a diary entry on May 17, "Miss Ima gives a garden party for River Oaks folks 5 to 7."

Unfortunately, exactly two weeks later on May 31, disaster struck when, following several days of torrential rains, the bayou rose out of its banks and waters flowed across Bayou Bend. Clean-up began the next day, and repairs continued throughout June and July as loads of topsoil were brought in and spread over the devastated lawns. The flood damaged a number of the old trees so cherished by the Hoggs, and one major aspect of the post-flood activity was a program to repair them, with seventy-five trees receiving attention from the Blume System. Ima was away for the summer but was kept up to date on developments in the gardens by H. E. Brigham, office manager for Hogg Brothers. By August, things had begun to return to normal and the garden staff was try-ing to get Bermuda grass started on the lawns. By September, the flood damage had for the most part been repaired.

That fall, even as the gardens in the near vicinity of the house were being developed, the attention to the edges of the gardens and the woods that had marked the activity before the Hoggs moved into Bayou Bend in November 1928 continued. The dogwood introduced earlier in the wooded area south of the house were augmented by thirty-eight more during late 1929 and early 1930. Always the hands-on gardener, Miss Hogg was very particular about the placement of transplanted dogwood, believing that each tree, in order to survive, needed to be oriented according to the compass direction of its original location. At the same time, forty-two double Reeves spirea and forty-two bridal wreath bushes (also a variety of spirea) as well as a number of cape jasmine gardenias were added in that area, indicating the importance of the natural woodlands to the overall concept of the garden.[59] The introduction of these white-flowering shrubs along with the dogwood, all staples of the antebellum garden, presaged the evolution of a white garden in the middle of the woods a few years later.

By 1930, Miss Hogg's garden notebooks reveal a pattern of ordering plant material from vendors around the country that would become a biannual, spring and fall activity for the next decade. Because roses were a staple of the antebellum garden and had been an important feature of the garden of Ima Hogg's grandmother Stinson, it is not surprising that by 1930 acquisition of roses became a major interest for Miss Hogg. Indeed, 210 bushes of five different varieties were introduced to Bayou Bend in March of that year. Her notebook entries from that fall list six varieties of "Old Time Roses" as well as fifteen tree roses.[60] It was typical of Miss Hogg that when she became interested in a subject, she acquired and read books to research her new interest. *The American Rose Annual 1930* was added to her library that same year. Published by the American Rose Society, the book contains various essays on roses and rose care and includes a chapter titled "The Best Roses For Texas," by an author from San Antonio who recommended five varieties. Two of those, 'Red Radiance' and 'Kaiserin Auguste Viktoria', had already been introduced into the garden at Bayou Bend.

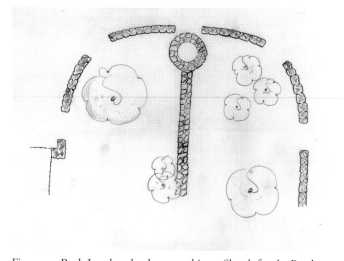

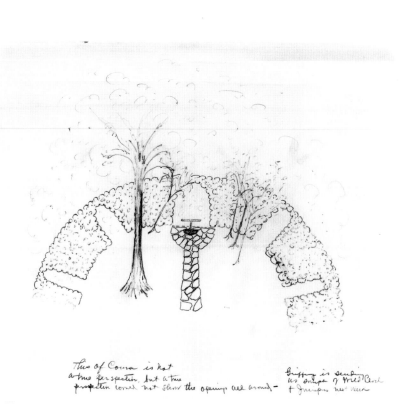

Figure 24. Ruth London, landscape architect. Sketch for the Peach Garden (now the terrace west of the Clio Garden). *Ima Hogg Papers, Center for American History, The University of Texas at Austin (CN11961).*

Figure 25. Ruth London, landscape architect. Another sketch for the Peach Garden. *Ima Hogg Papers, Center for American History, The University of Texas at Austin (CN11961).*

By the end of 1930, the gardens at Bayou Bend were well established. As we have seen, there were three major areas: the woodlands, the upper garden, and the lower garden. In the last two, the plant material was annuals, perennials, and bulbs with a palette that tended toward pink and white. In addition, there was a major planting of roses in a variety of colors in the lower garden. In the woodlands, native plants like holly, yaupon, and dogwood were augmented with crepe myrtle, cape jasmine gardenia, spirea, and bridal wreath, all popular antebellum plants that had been introduced from Asia to the American South in the nineteenth century. Several more years would pass, however, before two of the most quintessential antebellum plants, camellias and azaleas, also imports from the orient, would begin to assume an important role in Miss Hogg's garden at Bayou Bend.

## NEW GARDEN PLANS, NEW GARDEN PLANTS, 1931–34

During her first three years at Bayou Bend, Ima Hogg established a regular rhythm of garden care, ordering and planting annuals and perennials and augmenting existing plant material such as dogwood. In 1931, this routine altered when plans for the expansion of the gardens were

initiated. As with the first garden design, the new garden area was secluded from the primary north-south axis of the property. In the first phase, during the fall and winter of 1931–32, plans for a new "Peach Garden" at Bayou Bend were under way. Miss Hogg began to work in depth with Ruth London (1892–1966), a landscape architect associated with a newly established landscape design firm, Houston Studio Gardens. Although the firm had previously performed minor work, such as pruning roses, at Bayou Bend, a substantial payment of $61.25 to Houston Studio Gardens in October 1931 indicates that an important endeavor, such as design work, was undertaken.[61] The result of that work is documented by two surviving sketches (figures 24 and 25) that delineate a semicircular plan. The shape corresponds with the area at the bayou's edge, immediately west of the lower garden where today there is a raised brick terrace of the same shape, enclosed by a ligustrum hedge. The tree plan, featuring one large example at the upper left and a smaller one at the lower right, corresponds to the tree location in that area, and in one of the drawings, a building corner is indicated in the exact location of the northwest corner of the "Gardener's Cottage," the building adjacent to the parterre lower garden. Wild peach is mentioned in an inscription at the bottom of one drawing, and indeed at the end of the year

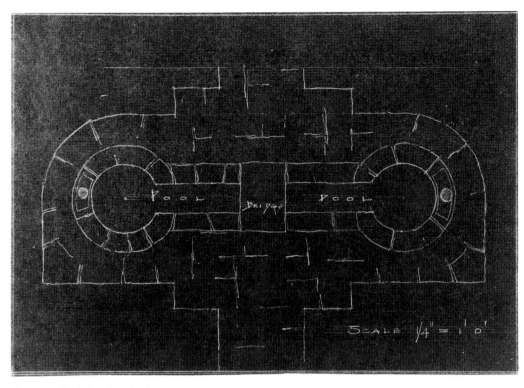

Figure 26. Ruth London, landscape architect. Sketch for the proposed Green Garden. *Ima Hogg Papers, Center for American History, The University of Texas at Austin.*

payment for drayage of fifty wild peach trees is documented in the Bayou Bend household accounts.[62]

The garden being developed was not simply a new garden space, but also an enclosed garden room, and was called the "Peach Garden." Its location was to the west of the parterre lower garden. The concept of a garden room, which represents an enclosed garden space, was new to garden design in the 1920s and represents a departure from the open, flat Victorian style of "bedding out" with patterns of color from massed annuals and perennials, seen in Bayou Bend's first unenclosed gardens. The Peach Garden, with its enclosing hedge of peach trees, was the first expression of this concept (which was later applied to the East Garden and Diana Lawn). Miss Hogg commissioned Ruth London to develop the garden room plan further, and in 1932 she produced two sketches, one a somewhat summary sketch (figure 26), the other a more finished plan (figure 27), in which the proposed improvement for the area is referred to as "Green Garden."[63]

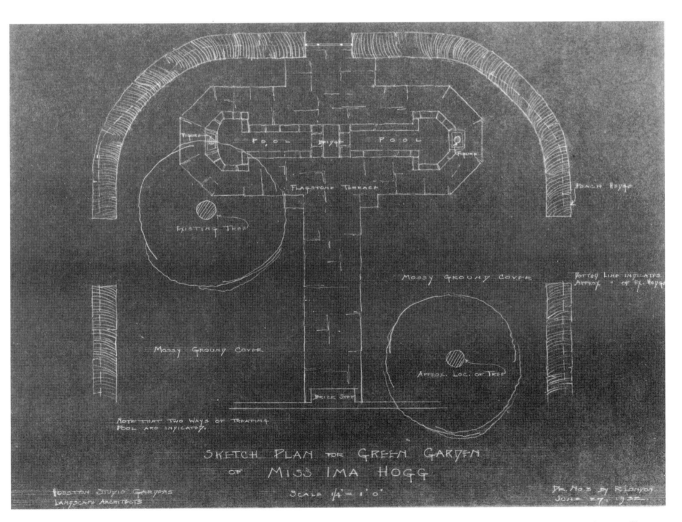

Figure 27. Ruth London, landscape architect. Sketch plan for Green Garden of Miss Ima Hogg. *Ima Hogg Papers, Center for American History, The University of Texas at Austin (CN11963).*

Although earlier scholarship suggested that these sketches are proposals for the upper or East Garden, there is compelling evidence that the designs are for the area west of the parterre lower garden that had been improved in late 1931.[64] First is the overall D shape and the location of the two large existing trees, all seen in the "Peach Garden"; second is the notation in the "Green Garden" drawing that indicates a peach hedge around the perimeter, clearly a holdover from the earlier improvements; third is the notation of a brick step at the bottom of the same drawing. At this point in the development of Bayou Bend's gardens, the use of brick was limited to the lower garden, and this noted step represents a transition to the new area. Indeed, today there is an identical brick step in that area. In contrast, in the upper or East Garden, the entrance from the adjacent terrace, which is flagstone, has no step but is all on one level.

Elements of London's scheme look both backward to the 1928 Hare and Hare proposal, and forward to developments that would be initiated several years later. The central walkway leading to an octagonal area closely echoes the northernmost part of the Hare and Hare proposal, which also featured lateral octagonal shapes at right angles to the paved approach. In London's 1932 plan, this layout may have stemmed from the simple paved path and birdbath of the "Peach Garden" sketches, and then been improved and formalized with ideas from the Hares. Most importantly, the "Green Garden" proposal calls for pools, introducing the element of water for the first time to the gardens at Bayou Bend. London returned to the motif of the formal, geometrically shaped pool surrounded by terracing when she undertook designs for revising the upper garden two years later.

Why Ruth London's June 1932 proposal for the "Green Garden" was not pursued is not known. However, two developments were most likely the contributing factors. Late in the summer of 1932, Houston was hit by a major hurricane and the gardens at Bayou Bend suffered serious damage. The subsequent need for major garden repairs in the wake of the hurricane undoubtedly dampened any enthusiasm for starting on a new garden at that moment. Also, Ima Hogg's health had taken a turn for the worse, and she was away from Houston for an extended period of time.[65]

Concurrent with the structural changes and improvements for the Bayou Bend garden during the early 1930s, a major change in plant material was under way. Bayou Bend is today famous for its azaleas and camellias, yet as we have seen, neither of these two plants was present in the garden at its earliest stages. Azaleas were introduced when seven were planted in the spring of 1930.[66] Although it is not known precisely who was the first person to bring azaleas to Houston, certainly Miss Hogg was among the very first. It is interesting to note that *A Garden Book for Houston,* published only one year earlier in 1929 by the Houston Forum of Civics, does not contain any mention of azaleas. In 1930, propagation of azaleas in Houston was new, experimental, and difficult because Houston's natural clay soil is entirely too alkaline for the azalea, which requires an acidic soil. The only solution was to change the soil entirely to achieve the proper degree of acidity. The small number of the first azalea planting at Bayou Bend suggests that they were likely an experiment. It appears that the experiment was successful, because two hundred fifty more azaleas were purchased in December 1931, at the same time that the wild peaches were bought for the new garden at the bayou's edge. Where these azaleas were planted is not indicated in the garden records, but there are suggestions that some may have been placed in the piney woods south of the house, and others were almost certainly planted around the upper garden, which only a year later was described as the azalea garden.[67]

Miss Hogg's library copy of a recently published book, *Azaleas and Camellias* by Harold Hume, purchased by her in March 1932, is marked with underlined passages and handwritten notes. In the section where Hume listed azalea varieties, those that attracted her attention were carefully annotated: a small "x" next to the Indicas and a dash next to the Kurumes. Other azalea names, such as 'Rosedown Pink', 'Mobile Orchid', 'Early Pink', and 'Elegans Superba' were written by Miss Hogg in the margin of the page, and she noted in parentheses that the last two were at Bellingrath Gardens in Mobile, Alabama.[68] At the same time, camellias from Louisiana were making their debut at Bayou Bend. The first arrived in the spring of 1932 and twelve more the following spring. Although Miss Hogg's notes do not indicate where the first camellias were planted, she recorded that the second lot were to be planted around the azalea garden.[69] As with the azaleas, the camellia section of Hume's book was also closely studied. Similarly, plants on the list of varieties that interested her were checked and the names of other varieties noted in the margins; the sections on planting and feeding were carefully studied and heavily underlined.

Although under medical treatment and away from Houston during this period, Miss Hogg made sure that these antebellum southern garden plants were added to Bayou Bend. Her thirst for news of the garden was a recurring theme in her letters home: "Did the violets live? How is the garden? Are the azaleas and camellias blooming yet? I wish I had gotten more dogwood . . . I suppose it is too late now." The faithful Mr. Brigham served as her eye, reporting developments in his frequent responses to letters. Typical was his observation passed on during the fall of 1933 that the recently introduced camellias and azaleas were doing well, that there would be a bumper crop of camellia blossoms, and that the azaleas were in full bud.[70]

The two major projects undertaken in the years between 1930 and 1934—the creation of a structured garden room by the edge of the bayou, and the introduction of camellias and azaleas, which were placed primarily in the area of the upper garden east of the house—laid the groundwork for even more ambitious developments during the next five years. Whereas the earlier changes to the design of the gardens at Bayou Bend were somewhat modest and incremental, what would follow was ambitious and was accomplished in two major campaigns.

## THE EAST GARDEN, WHITE GARDEN, AND SPECIALIZED CAMELLIAS, 1934–37

A new phase of extraordinary creative activity in Bayou Bend Gardens began in the late summer of 1934; it altered the design and character of the gardens forever. "Please tell OK nothing in the Upper Garden . . . is to be the same."[71] These prophetic words written by Miss Hogg summarize developments that culminated nearly a year later with the creation of a new garden room, laid out over the bones of the Caldwell design for the upper garden at the east end of the house. Heretofore the schemes for improvements had concentrated on the D-shaped area between the lower or Rose Garden and the bayou. Why attention shifted

from that location to the upper garden is not immediately obvious. However, the earlier, eccentrically shaped location was not very large and likely did not offer sufficient room for what Miss Hogg and Ruth London must have had in mind. A sketch by London (figure 28) suggests their dialogue on what might be. Included are revealing marginal comments such as, "Better shallow niches in hedge for statues so; is too Italian?" and "Wouldn't iron rail be better than low hedge here?"[72] The first comment hints at Miss Hogg's natural and continued resistance to formality as she and London worked out their ideas. By midsummer, those ideas for the new garden had coalesced to the degree that they could be formalized into a finished drawing (figure 29), titled "Design Plan for the Azalea Garden for Miss Ima Hogg River Oaks, Houston,"

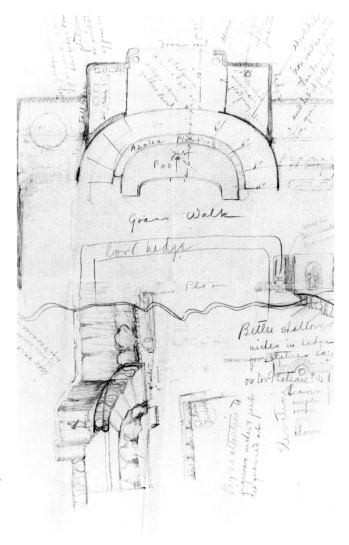

Figure 28. Ruth London, landscape architect. Sketch for the East Garden. *The Museum of Fine Arts, Houston, Archives.*

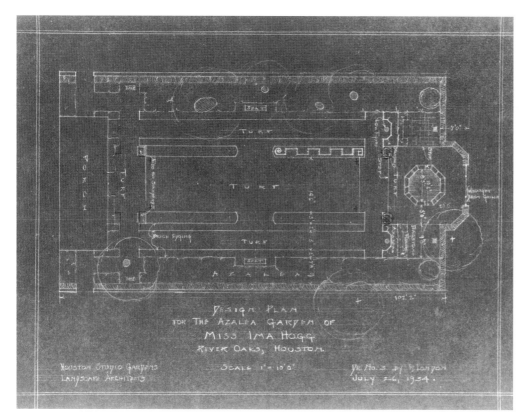

Figure 29. Ruth London, landscape architect. Design plan for the Azalea Garden of Miss Ima Hogg, River Oaks, Houston, 1934. *Ima Hogg Papers, Center for American History, The University of Texas at Austin (CN11964).*

Figure 30. The Upper Garden (now the East Garden) in the snow, showing the open expanses surrounding the area, c. 1930. *The Museum of Fine Arts, Houston, Archives.*

numbered 3 and dated July 26, 1934.[73] By August, London had staked out the new plan over the existing garden.

What Ruth London was creating was in part a continuation of ideas that had been proposed for the "Green Garden," an enclosed garden room with a geometric focal point at the end. The new garden was a great departure from the earlier scheme of the upper garden, where the beds had simply been laid out in an open space (figure 30), and as such represented a major step away from naturalism and toward formality for Bayou Bend. In the new plan, the area of the garden at the east end of the house is enclosed with an evergreen hedge delineating a formal, rectangular space the same width as the terrace and extending eastward from the terrace and porch to the edge of a ravine. The design retains the motif of lateral beds set within the carpet of green grass, and London's drawing suggests a scrolled Greek key motif, probably of clipped boxwood, within one of the beds. However, that very formal element was not realized and, instead, these beds continued to be planted with blue pansies and irises.[74] Vertically placed bricks provide crisp outlines for the lateral beds, and similar lines of brick within the flanking panels of grass carpet lead the eye to the east end, with its two statuary niches set within azaleas. Centered between them are two shallow brick steps leading up to a slightly raised area. There, the exedra shape of the earlier garden has been replaced by an enclosed rectangle with a central octagonal pool and fountain. Set within a hedge beyond the pool, wrought-iron gates, similar to the idea mentioned in the notes of the conceptual drawing, provide an opening and view of the ravine and woods beyond. The scroll-and-lyre-shape design of the wrought iron echoes that of the cast ironwork of the house. Flanking the grass terrace surrounding the pool are small, square, raised and paved spaces for seating furniture. Although the London plan called for these to be flagstone, echoing the terrace at the opposite end, they were made in the same soft pale pink antique brick of the nearby steps and borders within the grass panels. Within the hedge that delineates the sides of the garden room, London's plan called for beds of azaleas. When realized, these beds were planted in such a way that the pink blooms of the banked azaleas shaded from light to dark (figure 31). Outside the evergreen hedge which enclosed the garden room, London introduced a

Figure 31. In the East Garden, the
azaleas shade from light to dark pink.

Figure 32. Ima Hogg and Julia Ideson in the East Garden, c. 1936. *The Museum of Fine Arts, Houston, Archives.*

parallel planting of pink camellias.[75] Within the garden, at the middle of each of the lateral azalea beds, London designed a brick-paved inset for a garden bench (figure 32). The design for the hedge separating the main body of the garden from the raised section called for two niches for small ornamental sculptures, again echoing the idea noted on the early conceptual sketch. In the completed garden, a pair of lead figures of a boy and a girl were installed in the insets at the east end (figure 33).

The implementation of Ruth London's plan for Miss Hogg's Azalea Garden not only brought about a major change to the area of the old upper garden, but also served as the first stage in replacing the naturalistic, open, and informal qualities to the east and north of the house with highly structured and formal spaces. Additionally, two new formal elements were introduced: ornamental garden sculpture and a pool with fountain. These elements would become important features a few years later in the last major development of the gardens north of the house.

Figure 33. The East Garden.

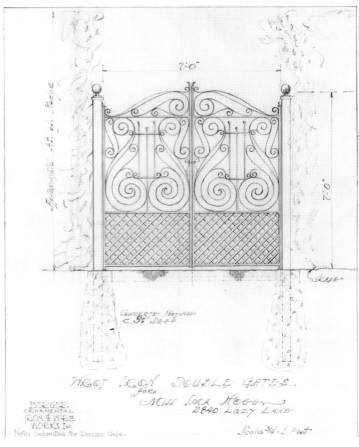

Figure 34. "Wrot Iron Double Gates for Miss Ima Hogg." Designed by Ruth London for Berger Ornamental Iron Works for the Lower Garden (now the Clio Garden). *Ima Hogg Papers, Center for American History, The University of Texas at Austin (CN11960).*

Figure 35. The iron gates installed in the Clio Garden.

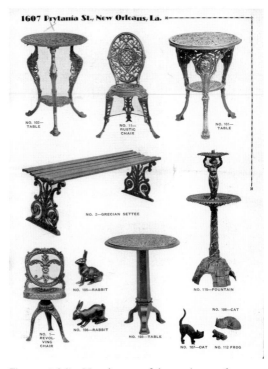

Figure 36. Miss Hogg's copy of the catalogue of Hinderer's Iron Works, New Orleans, illustrating the lyre-based bench purchased for Bayou Bend (middle left). *The Museum of Fine Arts, Houston, Archives.*

Figure 37. An iron lyre-back bench at Bayou Bend, ordered from Webber Iron Works.

Work on the new project began in the fall of 1934 and continued into the next spring. Although Ruth London was in charge as the designer, Ima Hogg was not a passive participant. Her responsibility seems to have been the acquisition of plant material, and throughout the fall and early winter she was in search of just the right yaupon for the hedge and was also seeking azaleas and camellias for the beds.[76] London, who was supervising the actual work, was responsible as well for the design of iron gates for this garden and a large pair flanking the D-shaped area in the lower garden (figures 34 and 35). She also acted as agent in purchasing garden furniture, corresponding with Hinderer's Iron Works in New Orleans throughout the spring. A number of lyre-based Grecian benches, a laurel-pattern settee, and also a rustic chair and settee were purchased. These are still in use today at Bayou Bend, as is the cast-iron furniture acquired the next year from Webber Iron Works in Houston (figures 36 and 37).[77] By early spring of 1935, the project was coming to a conclusion. The plant material selected and ordered by Miss Hogg from disparate sources had arrived and was installed. Chris Miller, the original contractor for the house, built the pool and flanking terraces and laid out the brickwork for the edg-

Figure 38. The waterfall below the East Garden.

Figure 39. The White Garden.

ing of the beds and small seating areas. Although the exact sequence of events is not entirely clear, at some point after its completion, the new garden pool began to leak water down the edge of the ravine at the east end of the garden. Miss Hogg, one who typically could make a positive out of a problem, had the leaking water from the pool channeled to create a cascading waterfall ending in a small round pool and surrounded by a rock garden (figure 38).

At the same time that she was planning the alterations to the East Garden, Miss Hogg was ordering white camel-

lias for another area; entries dated December 1934 in her garden notebook indicate that they were to be planted in both the "White Garden" and at the "entrance of the White garden" (figure 39). Although there had been earlier intimations of white-blooming plants being placed in the wooded area south of the house, including spirea, bridal wreath, and dogwood—seventy-eight more dogwood were purchased in March 1935—this is the first actual mention of a specific garden and the first use of the term White Garden. The concept of a white garden was not

Figure 40. 'Pink Perfection' camellia.

Figure 41. 'La Peppermint' camellia.

new to Ima Hogg or to Houston. As early as 1929, the Forum of Civics publication *A Garden Book for Houston* included a discussion of a white garden, noting, "In the languid heat of summer, how grateful to our senses is an enclosure frosty with silvery foliage and white flowers."[78]

By spring 1936, the new Azalea Garden at the east end of the house and the new White Garden in the deep wood, both complete, were revealed to the public for the first time. Two contemporary published accounts provide a wonderful picture of their appearance. A magazine article provides brief mention of Miss Hogg's new White Garden: "The gardens are very lovely, one being entirely white, with plantings of dogwood and white azaleas." A more comprehensive view of the improvements created in the Bayou Bend gardens over the previous two years appeared in the *Houston Post*:

*In the extensive grounds of Miss Ima Hogg's home, many developments of unusual beauty and interest are to be seen. In the rustic, woodsy section, there are dogwood and massed plantings of azaleas in separate colors, pink and white, with great drifts of hyacinths and daffodils at their base. There is an intriguing rock garden and waterfall on a certain slope. A gorgeous hedge of Perfection Pink [sic] Camellias shares its glory with a number of other camellias of various types. But above all, and presenting a picture that will long be remembered, is the formal Garden. Enclosed by a hedge and a fence of antique ornamental iron work of rare beauty, this garden is unsurpassed in perfection of design and color. Wide banks of pink azaleas shading from pale to deep tones, beds of blue pansies and Dutch irises all blend in a harmony of exquisite loveliness.[79]*

This precise account of the new Azalea Garden's layout and appearance provides a vivid image of what Miss Hogg and Ruth London had created. In describing the new garden as "formal," the writer underscores the contrast to the garden area previously discussed, which was characterized as "woodsy," and indicates how far Miss Hogg had come from the informal naturalism of the old upper garden. Additionally we are provided a more complete picture of the woodland garden, which included not only dogwood but also azaleas of several colors and an extensive amount

of spring bulbs. The mention of the Pink Perfection hedge both gives a fuller view of the camellia plantation in the woods and clearly describes a hedge along a woodland path between the White Garden and lawn south of the house, where today there still is a hedge of these camellias adjacent to the major concentration of camellias in the woodland garden (figures 40 and 41).

The following year ushered in a period of further, even more extensive additions to the camellia collection. Miss Hogg's visit in early 1937 to the Camellia Show in Lafayette, Louisiana, may have sparked this activity, as very soon after she was in correspondence with a number of vendors making inquiries about the availability of specific camellia plants.[80] One was E. A. McIlhenny, whom she visited at his plantation on Avery Island, Louisiana, in March. Edward Avery McIlhenny (1872–1949), a renowned naturalist and horticulturist, had established a business there known as Jungle Gardens, to grow and sell specimen plants. He had provided her some grafted camellias a few months earlier, and after her visit she ordered eight prize *Camellia japonica* bushes to be delivered the following November. Miss Hogg's preferred color palette was pink and white and of the new selection, half the order included three of the former and one of the latter. Interestingly, however, four of the McIlhenny camellias chosen by her were in tones of red. At this same time McIlhenny was developing a special camellia just for her. This he named 'Missima', and in writing to Miss Hogg, he noted, "I am so glad to know that you will make a feature in your garden of MISSIMA. I believe this camellia is destined to be one of the most favored when it is better known; first on account of its delicate color and shape; second because it bears its flowers on very long stems, making it suitable for vase-cutting." The variegated white and pink 'Missima' was propagated later that year, and McIlhenny wrote, "Regarding Missima camellias—the grafts have done remarkably well and I can make shipment at any time you see fit."[81] What became of the 'Missima' camellias sent to Bayou Bend is a mystery, for they totally disappeared, and garden records make no further mention of them. Recently, however, a variety bearing the name was located in Florida and a number of the plants were shipped to Houston and flourish once again in the gardens at Bayou Bend.

## THE FINAL PHASE: THE DIANA, CLIO, AND EUTERPE GARDENS, 1937–39; THE BUTTERFLY GARDEN, 1940

Even as Miss Hogg was actively in pursuit of new specimen camellias, she was also making plans for an additional project, to alter the expansive, sloping lawn north of the house. This project eventually became quite extensive, bringing about the most sweeping change to the garden's design and character in its history. Developments and improvements in other Houston gardens seem to have been undertaken between 1937 and 1939 in anticipation of the annual meeting of the Garden Club of America, held in Houston during late February and early March 1939.[82] The impending arrival in Houston of distinguished gardeners from all over the country probably also provided the impetus for Miss Hogg to embark on an ambitious new garden at Bayou Bend.

Beginning in the spring of 1937, the focus at Bayou Bend shifted from the woodland gardens and the two original gardens, all hidden from view off the main axis of the site, to the broad, tree-studded expanse of lawn located north of the house on axis with the central hall. Despite statements made in the 1980s by landscape designer C. C. "Pat" Fleming that, at Bayou Bend's inception, this area was a thicket of woods and underbrush extending all the way up the hill to the flagstone terrace, a pre-1937 photograph reveals that it was simply an open lawn punctuated by those large, picturesque trees saved by the Hoggs a decade earlier (see figure 16).[83] That spring the natural slope of the lawn was reworked and recontoured to step down in three levels to the flat area at the bottom of the hill. The garden wall, on the western perimeter of the area was raised approximately four feet to accommodate the new stepped contour.[84]

In June, Miss Hogg, en route to a summer in Europe, sent instruction to Brigham: "Just a few words about the garden. There are some vines to be planted against the

Figure 42. The north lawn showing the newly terraced slope and raised garden wall. *The Museum of Fine Arts, Houston, Archives.*

Figure 43. Two views of the north lawn after spring 1939. *The Museum of Fine Arts, Houston, Archives.*

wall on the terrace side. Begin at the bed near the house (on the stone terrace). I bought some 'fig vines' . . . They should be planted . . . three feet apart and fertilized with dairy fertilizer and bone meal." Later correspondence between them discusses the new hedging between the rose garden and the lawn.[85] These disparate pieces of information, when taken together, provide an important picture of what had been completed by June 1937: the recontouring of the lawn into grassy terraces, the raising of the garden wall, and the introduction of hedging to enclose the newly worked space (figures 42 and 43). Thus it is clear that by that time, the outlines of a new garden room had been set out on the open, sloping lawn north of the house. This timing is important, because historically the entire scheme for the north lawn garden room has been ascribed to the Houston landscape firm of C. C. "Pat" Fleming and Albert Sheppard. As we shall see presently, Fleming and Sheppard first came to Bayou Bend seven months later.

By July 1937, Miss Hogg, then in Florence, visited the studio of Antonio Frilli, a firm that specialized in marble statuary and garden furniture. Later she wrote Brigham that she was thinking about some statues for the garden. Frilli provided price estimates to Miss Hogg for a replica of the Diana of Versailles, Verrocchio's fountain figure of a boy holding a fish, Roman style vases, and garden benches. Additionally Frilli indicated that he would provide green marble bases for the statues. Letters that followed indicate that Ima Hogg was determined to pin down Frilli to the best deal that could be arranged. A series of offers and counteroffers between the two ensued. She finally asked Frilli to quote a price in U.S. dollars for the statue of Diana and a green marble pedestal. She also asked him to give her the size and thickness of the green marble and to supply her with a sample of it.[86] Concurrently, Ima Hogg was comparison shopping at Marino Baroni, another Florentine firm that dealt in garden statuary. Under discussion with Baroni were a replica of the same Diana and also one of the Apollo Belvedere. However, by the end of the summer the process was coming to a resolution and she wrote Brigham, "I hope to have one beautiful statue which will at any event not be in Houston until I get there to inspect it."[87] The Frilli firm ultimately prevailed, and in September, having returned to America,

Miss Hogg sent Frilli a personal check for $384.10, approximately one-third of the agreed-upon cost for the figure of Diana.[88]

Miss Hogg's decision to purchase the classical white marble statue of the Diana of Versailles, virtually life size, indicates an important philosophical change for her garden, even if at that moment she was not fully cognizant of the fact that she was moving away from the simple naturalism that had heretofore prevailed. The addition of such a figure to the Bayou Bend garden, in fact, introduced an inherent element of formality that, with the exception of the new garden room designed by Ruth London, had not previously existed. The use of sculpture in Miss Hogg's garden was not without precedent, although what was previously used was completely different in character. In the late 1920s, a nineteenth-century wooden trade figure representing an Indian princess was placed as decoration in the wooded area of the garden during the spring (figure 44). There also was the suggestion for statuary at either

Figure 44. In the late 1920s, a nineteenth-century wooden trade figure of an Indian princess was placed as decoration in the wooded area of the garden. *The Museum of Fine Arts, Houston, Archives.*

Figure 45. Alinari photograph of Euterpe, the Muse of Music. *The Museum of Fine Arts, Houston, Archives.*

and the Continents were introduced in the 1830s.[89] By the 1930s, Rosedown and its garden represented a remarkably intact survival of the antebellum period, and it is extremely likely that Miss Hogg was familiar with what was there; thus, in her quest to create a neo-antebellum garden, she would have been aware of a nineteenth-century precedent for the use of classical statuary. Closer to home, classical statuary had already been introduced into two Houston gardens. At Hugh Roy Cullen's 1933 house, Azalea Court, architect John Staub designed not only the house but, concurrently, the garden. Two life-sized white marble statues of classical figures—Venus, the goddess of love, and Hebe, the goddess of youth—were used at Azalea Court as focal points where the major and secondary axes crossed. In the spring of 1935, just two years prior to Miss Hogg's purchase of Diana, Mr. and Mrs. John E. Green, neighbors on Lazy Lane, had acquired two large antique statues of Roman centurions that had originally been in an old Italian garden.[90]

What developed next, during the fall of 1937, is difficult to reconstruct. We do know that work on the terracing, raising the wall, and the new hedges had been accomplished by the beginning of the summer. Whether Ruth London was involved is not clear, but a $60 payment to her in June, at the same time as the payments for the terracing of the lawn and raising of the garden wall, suggests that she had consulted on these initial stages of the project. Why London was not retained to continue as the major designer for the new garden remains a mystery, but for some reason she was not. Houston Studio Gardens had by then closed its doors and London was out on her own without the resources and support of that organization, and this may have been a contributing factor to her limited activity at Bayou Bend between June 1937 and February 1938, when she totally ceased to have any involvement.[91] At any rate, after her return to Houston in September 1937, it seems that Miss Hogg was basically on her own to figure out how to proceed. She considered the question during that fall. Correspondence with Frilli, inquiring about the delivery date of Diana, also asks about copies of other statues, intimating that something much more complex than the simple placement of Diana was in mind. Frilli responded that Diana had been shipped from Livorno on October 20. In the same letter he

end of the pools in Ruth London's unrealized scheme for a Green Garden; and, as part of the new formal azalea garden designed by Ruth London, the two small lead figures of a chubby boy and girl were placed as accents against the low hedge at the east end. The American trade figure and these cute little figures were a far cry, however, from the noble statue just purchased by Miss Hogg.

The use of classical marble statuary was a feature, though a rare one, of the finest antebellum southern gardens, such as Rosedown in St. Francisville, Louisiana, where white Carrara marble figures of the Four Seasons

Figure 46. Alinari photograph of Calliope, the Muse of Poetry. *The Museum of Fine Arts, Houston, Archives.*

Figure 47. Alinari photograph of classical sculpture in the Vatican museum. Left to right: Clio, the Muse of History; Urania, the Muse of Astronomy; and Thalia, the Muse of Comedy. *The Museum of Fine Arts, Houston, Archives.*

assured Miss Hogg that he could make "authentic copies of any sculpture in the museums of Florence and Rome."[92] The next month he sent her photos of statuary in the Vatican Museum. Miss Hogg, with her vast musical background—she trained as a concert pianist and was a founder of the Houston Symphony Society in 1913—was, not surprisingly, immediately attracted to Euterpe, the Muse of Music. However, as the figure is seated, rather than standing, as is more common in classical sculpture, finding a mate for her would prove to be a problem. Frilli suggested a "Personaggio Romano," but after considering Calliope, the Muse of Poetry, who is also seated, Miss Hogg selected another seated figure, Clio, the Muse of History, which reflected another of her interests and enthusiasms (figures 45–47). At the same time, Frilli and Miss Hogg also conferred about the acquisition of white marble garden urns. The figure of Diana arrived in December 1937 and the next month Miss Hogg sent the final payment of $766.

Immediately after the turn of the new year, 1938, Miss Hogg's daily diaries and appointment books indicate that she was deeply involved with plans for the garden, making diverse inquiries such as the availability of antique brick or the specific height of cedars, as well as placing orders for azaleas and camellias. Her appointment book for January 15, 1938, bears the notation: "Mrs. Shipman garden plans" and her diary for the same day records Mrs. Ellen Biddle Shipman's New York address and telephone number. The reference to Ellen Biddle Shipman, the renowned landscape architect based in New York, confirms the oral tradition that Shipman was involved with the design of the garden at Bayou Bend. On February 12, Miss Hogg sent Shipman a check for $106 as payment for the consultation. The diary bears two other important notations: for January 22, exactly a week after Shipman's visit to Bayou Bend: "Fleming 11:30" and the telephone number "J 22100" and for January 27, "Mr. Fleming."[93] These entries are significant to sorting out not only exactly when Fleming and Sheppard, who have traditionally been ascribed as authors of the entire Diana Garden terraces and reflecting pool, became involved, but also the extent of their creative contribution. Late in life Pat Fleming related his version of the story in an interview with the author.[94]

Figure 48. Uncrating the sculpture of Diana, winter 1938. *The Museum of Fine Arts, Houston, Archives.*

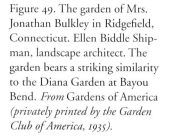

Figure 49. The garden of Mrs. Jonathan Bulkley in Ridgefield, Connecticut. Ellen Biddle Shipman, landscape architect. The garden bears a striking similarity to the Diana Garden at Bayou Bend. *From* Gardens of America *(privately printed by the Garden Club of America, 1935).*

Three major factors of Fleming's story appear to be lacking in fact. First, that the "thicket" or woods came right up the slope to the edge of the north terrace of the house; second, that he told Miss Hogg about the statue of Diana; and third, that the firm was involved from the outset. We have already seen that the area north of the house was not a thicket but sloping lawn. We also know that the statue of Diana was already at Bayou Bend in December, a month before Fleming's appointment in late January. Interviews in the mid-1990s with Albert Sheppard give a clear picture and confirm the time frame indicated by Miss Hogg's diary, an initial telephone call followed five days later by a visit to Bayou Bend by Fleming. The first contact was made, Sheppard recalled, after the firm had opened new offices in the River Oaks Shopping Center in December of 1937: "Miss Ima called our office one day and wanted to see us. I was working on a plan that had to be finished, so Pat went. He came back and told me about the statue still there in the crate. I saw it the next day" (figure 48). In answer to an inquiry as to whether Fleming had found the statue for Miss Hogg as he alleged, Sheppard responded, "Pat had not heard about any statue of Diana or any other statue that Miss Ima had seen or heard about. She did not talk to us and we did not know anything about one until the day she phoned us and Pat went to see her. We saw the statue then."[95]

Ima Hogg often sought advice from multiple sources when she had a difficult problem—in this case the newly improved landscape and the question of how to deal with the statue already at hand and possibly other statues as well. She had since the early 1930s turned to Ruth London for garden design. As we have seen, London was apparently involved prior to June and payments made to her for service in November and January suggest approximately seven hours' further consultation. As London seems not to have come up with the necessary input, Ima Hogg needed to look elsewhere. Shipman was one source.

During the 1930s, Ellen Biddle Shipman made annual winter tours through the South, giving lectures and consulting on gardens. To announce her tour, she published a

Figure 50. Sketch for the Diana Garden. It is not known whether this undated sketch is by Ima Hogg or Ellen Biddle Shipman. *Courtesy of Sally Robert Banttari.*

made an important transition between the formal garden and the woodland beyond it. At the same time as her visit to Bayou Bend, Shipman was working on a garden at Duke University, a major feature of which was steps down a terraced hill to a pool which formed the transition to a woodland beyond. The stepped terraces at Bayou Bend, which already existed when Shipman came to visit, may have actually been the idea of Miss Hogg herself. Her 1908 diary made while living in Berlin described a sleighing outing: " We went by way of Bismarck Allée which is lined with beautiful residences, some of which have large gardens, One I remember had terraces, four or five facing the river . . . and the effect was quite lovely."[98] The situation at Bayou Bend, with a series of grassy terraces descending toward the bayou, is certainly analogous. However, the idea for adding brick-lined steps set within the sloping grass between the terraces is very likely Shipman's. Thus, while Shipman did not actually make any plan for the

small brochure that included a listing of her charges for such consultations. Her first visit to Houston occurred in 1935, when she was invited to lecture under the aegis of the River Oaks Garden Club and the Garden Club of Houston; there is a strong possibility that Miss Hogg met Shipman at that time. Miss Hogg's January 1938 diary notation and payment the next month confirm a contemporary newspaper item, which noted that Shipman had been in Houston at that time conferring with Miss Ima Hogg about revising her garden.[96]

While it is not entirely clear what came of Shipman's consultation, there is a strong indication that she conceived the idea of where to place the statue of Diana and likely suggested the cross-axis locations for the other two, as yet undelivered, figures. The final placement of Diana, within a niche in the woods with a reflecting pool—strikingly similar to one worked out by Shipman for a garden designed for Mrs. Jonathan Bulkley in Ridgefield, Connecticut, in the late 1920s (figure 49)—is undoubtedly Shipman's. In the Bulkley garden she had carved an opening in the woods to create a woodland backdrop, also for a sculpture of Diana, in front of which was placed a reflecting pool. The statue was surrounded by low, flowering bushes and a screen of cypress was set behind.[97] Just as at Bayou Bend, Shipman's design for Mrs. Bulkley

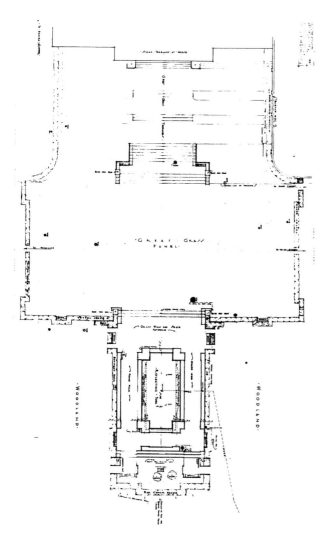

Figure 51. Plan of the Reflecting Pool for Miss Ima Hogg by Fleming and Sheppard, landscape architects, 1938. *Courtesy of Sally Robert Banttari.*

Diana Garden and stepped terraces at Bayou Bend, it seems safe to say that she contributed some distinctive details to the scheme—the steps, niche in the woods, reflecting pool, sculpture on axis, and a screen of trees beyond. The general ideas that had begun to crystallize for Miss Hogg are suggested by an undated, rough sketch that clearly shows the basic outlines of the garden (figure 50). Whether the sketch is by Miss Hogg's or Shipman's hand is not known. It does, however, clearly provide the starting point for the work by Fleming and Sheppard that would ensue. Undoubtedly the original plan by Hare and Hare also contributed to the final design of the Diana Garden.

Albert Sheppard's narrative of the events in January 1938 continued:

*Pat got the plan of the property and I started laying out our first ideas during the next few days. Diana was the main accent for our plan . . . and the cross axis was located with the rose garden on one side and whatever at the other end . . . The thicket [niche in the woods at the north end of the lawn] had been cut. She called us to locate it [Diana]. They, Diana and the reflecting pool evolved simultaneously . . . We placed Diana as far from the house as the terrain would allow . . . [The] ideas [of the two other figures] existed simultaneously with the placement of Diana even though the statues had not been selected . . . Miss Ima's dealings with the sculptures in Italy indicated we would base the statues on the cross axis.*

As fate would have it, the original Fleming and Sheppard drawings for the Bayou Bend project have been lost, making it difficult to reconstruct the scope of their work. The one surviving is a reproduction made when the Bayou Bend drawings were still in Fleming's possession (figure 51).[99] It shows the entire area from the flagstone terrace of the house down the grass slope—described as "Great Grass Terraces"—across the flat "Great Green Grass Panel" to the reflecting pool and the Diana installation beyond. The drawing in fact represents a formalization of the shapes seen in the pencil sketch. What is tantalizing is that the drawing is labeled "Plan of the Reflecting Pool for Miss Ima Hogg," yet the rendering of the area around the reflecting pool is no more detailed

than that elsewhere in the drawing. Does this mean that Fleming and Sheppard only designed the reflecting pool area? Much of the evidence we have seen would indicate that is so, but the reality is likely not quite that simple. Whereas the niche in the woods and reflecting pool were Shipman's idea, certainly the details of the design and execution were by Fleming and Sheppard. Additionally, the realization of the steps on the already existing terraced slope, which carry out a suggestion that likely came from Shipman and echo the Hare and Hare design made ten years earlier, was undoubtedly made under Fleming and Sheppard's supervision (figure 52).

The surviving Fleming and Sheppard drawing indicates the large existing trees situated in unexpected locations, including a large oak in the midst of the lower set of steps. All but one of these trees would ultimately be retained. The drawing also shows the location of six marble benches and four monumental marble urns, which, as early as December 1937, Miss Hogg had been discussing with Frilli. These added a further note of formality and classicism to the garden. Their location, according to Sheppard, was determined by Miss Hogg herself. Fleming and Sheppard's scheme masterfully uses soft old brick set vertically in the ground to delineate the grass steps and the edges of the beds in the reflecting pool area, lending an overall note of crispness that echoes the clear, classical lines of Staub's house. The use of single lines of vertical brick to delineate the beds around the reflecting pool is very similar to Ruth London's treatment in the azalea garden three years earlier. London's design may have been the inspiration, or perhaps the motif was repeated to provide a visual link between the two formal gardens.

Once Diana's location was determined, Sheppard recalled, there were no problems in working out the rest of the proposed scheme. The central circle of the parterre Rose Garden became the location of a new circular brick pedestal for one of the other sculptures, ultimately Clio, and a spot on axis to the east of the "Great Grass Panel" the site for a new pedestal for the second sculpture, Euterpe. That area, which the surviving drawing labels as woodland, had been partially cleared for footpaths that ran through it. For the project, Sheppard related, the remaining underbrush was cleared. The siting for the

Figure 52. The grass terraces of the
north lawn under construction.
*The Museum of Fine Arts, Houston,
Archives.*

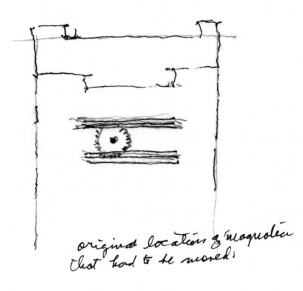

*original location of magnolia
that had to be moved.*

ALBERT SHEPPARD
SEP. 11 1996.

Figure 53. Sketch of the original location of the magnolia tree that
was cut down, by Albert Sheppard.

pedestal on which Euterpe would rest was dictated by the
presence of a large double-trunk sycamore on one side and
a towering single pine tree on the other. Once again, the
Hogg family's reverence for existing trees played a role in
the garden design. On the terraced steps that reverence
was also challenged. However, in this case the desire to retain trees was treated with rationality. Sheppard recalled
that there was one lone magnolia virtually on axis between
the garden facade's front door and the proposed location
of the reflecting pool (figure 53). All agreed that it had to
go. When the time came for the deed, Sheppard recounted, Miss Hogg was right out there with the work-
men, but appeared to be very unhappy, standing on one
foot and then another, her jaw firmly clenched. He told
her that if she wanted to change her mind and spare the
tree, it would be alright. "No," she replied, "it has to come
out, but it just feels to me like someone is pulling out one
of my teeth."[100]

One of the most difficult problems in the project was
determining what kind of tree would be used as a screen
behind Diana. Sheppard recalls that Miss Hogg toyed
with the idea of a screen of pink magnolia and, in fact, she
and the two young landscape architects made a motoring

trip over to Louisiana looking for nice vertical examples which would give just the right classical effect. By November 1938 Miss Hogg was in contact with McIlhenny, asking about Japanese yew which she told him she wanted as background for a marble figure. She indicated she desired compact and full trees, thirty-eight in total, at heights of eight, ten, and twelve feet. The variation in height would lend itself to a more picturesque and naturalistic effect. McIlhenny countered with the suggestion of *Ligustrum gracilis.* Ultimately they found the perfect solution, a group of cypress trees located in an old cemetery in New Braunfels, Texas. These were duly purchased and trucked to Houston (figure 54). By April 1938 Miss Hogg wrote Frilli that the statue of Diana was in place (figure 55), but there were problems with the green marble base.[101]

At the end of May, progress on the new garden was tellingly described by Miss Hogg in a letter to McIlhenny, in which she reveals the tension between her innate inclination to informality and naturalism and the new direction of formality that had evolved following the purchase of the classical sculpture of Diana: "My garden which I am making on the Bayou side of the house is coming along nicely and slowly. I hope you will like it. I am afraid it has changed the aspect of my place a great deal. Certainly it is on the formal side, which I had not originally intended."[102] This concern over the new formality may have been the reason she was not yet ready to make a decision on the two other sculptures. Although Frilli urged her to make her selection, she wrote him in late May that she was not ready to decide on the two statues but that he would hear from her in due time. As it turned out, this delay made it impossible for the sculptures to be delivered in time for the Garden Club of America annual meeting. The final decision was postponed until the fall, when she wrote Frilli that she had not ordered the statues because she wanted him to quote her a lower price that would include delivery to Houston. By that time, the spring 1939 visit of the Garden Club of America was looming for Miss Hogg. Letters gave way to cables as she wired Frilli at the end of October, ordering sculptures of Euterpe and Clio (rather than Calliope) and expressing the wish that they be delivered in Houston by the middle of February, indicating that the time frame was imperative because of the Garden Club meeting at the end of that month. Frilli wired back confirming the order, the February delivery, and the final price of $1,935.[103]

One major problem remained, however. As the originals of the two sculptures were in the collection of the Vatican Museum, Frilli was required to secure the Vatican's permission to reproduce them. In December the permission was granted, but with several important conditions. The casts from the originals would be made one at a time; a tax of 100,000 lire would be charged for the cast of Clio; and because Euterpe had not previously been cast, a second cast would be made for the Vatican Museum at Ima Hogg's expense. Miraculously, the casts were made and the sculptures (figure 56) were completed by mid-February, when Frilli wrote Miss Hogg that they were in the port of Livorno awaiting the next steamer.[104] However, the timing of Miss Hogg's order was not sufficient to meet the required delivery date in Houston before the last days of February, and the two Muses, Clio and Euterpe, did not arrive in Houston until April, two months after the Garden Club meeting (figure 57).

Throughout 1938, as Miss Hogg was working out the design of the new garden with Fleming and Sheppard and deciding on the two other sculptures, she was also actively involved in securing plant material for the new garden room. What she had in mind were old, large, and impressive examples that would provide a virtually instant sense of age for the new space. McIlhenny was a major source. During the spring she ordered six large, seven-to-eight-foot-tall 'Elegans' (an Indica azalea with light pink blossoms), and during the summer she ordered a number more. By December 1938 the material from McIlhenny began to arrive. Concurrently, large orders from other sources such as Kiyono in Mobile, Howards's Montopolis Nursery, and Houston's own Japanese Nursery were being delivered. Two engineering feats took up much of Fleming and Sheppard's time in the months leading up to the Garden Club meeting. One was the creation of an arching fountain in which jets of water would rise up out of the reflecting pool and frame the figure of Diana. It was difficult to get just the right water pressure to make the jets rise in a simple line and fall to the other side without undue splashing. In conjunction with the fountain, Miss

Figure 55. View of the Diana Fountain showing the original, green marble pedestal. *Ima Hogg Papers, Center for American History, The University of Texas at Austin (CN01709).*

Figure 56. The replica figure of Clio in progress at Frilli studio, Florence, 1939. *The Museum of Fine Arts, Houston, Archives.*

Figure 57. The empty pedestal prior to the delivery of the Euterpe statue. *The Museum of Fine Arts, Houston, Archives.*

Hogg wanted to have night lighting on the water jets and also in the surrounding trees. While the idea seems simple today, the technology for underwater lighting did not exist then, so Sheppard had to extemporize. Similarly, lighting for trees was unknown. Miss Hogg was quite sure of the effect she wanted to achieve, but found it difficult to express. Sheppard recalls that over a period of a month they came out at night with lamps and ladders, working by trial and error on various arrangements and effects. Miss Hogg was always there to supervise and critique.

At last the momentous occasion arrived, and on February 28, 1939, attendees at the Garden Club of America's Houston meeting began their three-day program. At the end of the second day, two moonlit teas were scheduled, one at the house of Mrs. Harry C. Wiess, and the other at the home of Miss Ima Hogg.[105] Miss Hogg invited Pat Fleming and Albert Sheppard to be on hand for the 6:30 event, the only men in attendance. The weather was not totally benign as there was a fine, misty rain falling. The ladies entered the house and because of the weather mostly stayed inside, but a few ventured outside where they were greeted by the sweep of the terraced lawn, the lighted Diana, and the dramatically floodlit trees. The

mist added a mysterious quality to the night scene, providing a romantic sense of antiquity to the newly created garden. Sheppard recalled that the sight was greeted by cries of delight by the first few who ventured outside. Those cries attracted the attention of all the others who then came out to see what was going on.

The gardens on tour during the Garden Club meeting were each described and illustrated in a book specially prepared for the annual meeting; both architects and garden designers were noted. Bayou Bend was credited to both Birdsall Briscoe and John Staub, the gardens to Ruth London and Fleming and Sheppard. The reason William Caldwell was not mentioned may stem from the fact that his upper garden had been obliterated by London's later garden room and his lower garden modified by Fleming and Sheppard. Why Shipman did not receive any mention may reflect the generosity of Miss Hogg in wanting to assure the reputation of the young men who helped her create the garden's final stage. What is apparent, however, is that over the years, Ima Hogg herself played the central role in the design and creation of the gardens at Bayou Bend. The description in the Garden Club book provides a vivid picture of Bayou Bend's appearance at that pivotal

moment in its history when the efforts begun in the early 1930s had been completed and Bayou Bend was entering its mature state as a great southern garden: "The classic portico and terrace of the lovely Latin Colonial house face upon the extensive garden of Diana. This semi-formal garden was constructed as a setting for the exquisite marble statue and has a fine background planting of Howard's hybrids and Elegans azaleas. The large reflecting pool is bordered with bands of ivy enclosed with English box hedges and Gardenia radicans." The description moves on to Ruth London's East Garden: "A formal garden, planted with salmon pink azaleas, blue pansies and iris overlooks a deep ravine with a small waterfall." The lower garden and woodlands are discussed: "A formal rose garden provides a view of the bayou bend. Throughout the native woods are hundreds of redbud and dogwood trees, azaleas and a profusion of naturalized bulbs."[106]

The description of the gardens at Bayou Bend reflects the culmination of more than two years' effort on the part of Miss Hogg to create her garden "on the bayou side," as she had described it a year earlier to McIlhenny. Fleming and Sheppard had been working at Bayou Bend for roughly a year. Ima Hogg was very much a hands-on client with this project, as she was with the 1934–35 project with Ruth London, and she made herself responsible for securing the plant material. The resultant garden, Sheppard correctly noted, was a cooperative effort between Miss Hogg and the landscape architects. The new space became the dominant feature of the gardens at Bayou Bend, the garden that ever after would always be photographed to represent Bayou Bend. The garden as it was in 1938, with its gnarled trees scattered randomly within the formal terraced space, had a curious tension between the formal and the informal. The presence of the ancient

trees, seemingly in the wrong places, provided a wonderful subliminal suggestion that nature had taken over a once pristine formal garden which in more recent years was reclaimed (figure 58). For Miss Hogg's new garden room this feature added both visual interest and a sense of history. While it is now clear that Fleming and Sheppard's role was far more limited than had been previously thought, there is no doubt that, although they did not conceive or design the space, they used their considerable talents to bring the ideas of others to reality; in that process, their first private garden project, they gained an expertise and level of taste that enabled them to design three other gardens by the time of the February/March 1939 Garden Club meeting in Houston. Later that year, in September 1939, Europe had plunged into yet another world war, an event that would both spell an end, all over America, to the development of gardens on the scale of

Miss Hogg's great southern garden at Bayou Bend and bring the Country House era to a close.

The winds of war had not yet reached America, however, and in the fall of 1940 the last of Bayou Bend's pre-war gardens was begun. Although Pat Fleming's account of this garden involves an extensive plan for the two areas flanking the drive south of the house, Albert Sheppard's recollection is quite different. Rather than a vast scheme, it was in fact a small, modest project, intended to be a sort of capriccio, nestled in an opening at the edge of the woods southeast of the house. Fleming, in fact, was not even involved. The design, in the shape of a spread-wing butterfly, was laid out on the ground by Fred Eckert, the brick mason who had worked on the Diana Garden and built the pedestals for Clio and Euterpe. Miss Hogg and Albert Sheppard advised as Eckert outlined the shape of the wings and antenna with bricks inserted vertically in the ground.[107] This technique echoes both the design used in Ruth London's Azalea Garden and that of Fleming and Sheppard in the Diana Garden and once again provided a visual link between this new garden and its predecessors. Nine courses of pavers formed the body. In its original prewar state, the butterfly was planted with low flowers, purple and yellow pansies, hyacinths and snow drops for color and ribs of "Chinese grass."[108] At some point after the war, the informal planting of low annuals was replaced with a more formal one of Kurume azaleas of differing colors and low bordering Japanese boxwood that we see today (figure 59). In doing this, Miss Hogg created a parterre that echoes the treatment in the Clio Garden which, following the replacement of the traditional roses there, also featured azaleas set within boxwood hedges. The different shades of pink azaleas, used to create the stripes of the butterfly's wings, recall the use of changing colors in the nearby Azalea, or East, Garden.

## THE LATE YEARS, 1941–65; A PUBLIC GARDEN, 1966–2004

During World War II, activity in the gardens at Bayou Bend was, understandably, kept at a minimal, maintenance level. From 1943 to 1946 Miss Hogg was served as a director of the Garden Club of America for Zone IX and was also a member of the board nominating committee. In 1959 the Garden Club of America awarded her prestigious national recognition in the form of the Amy Angell Collier Montague Medal given for outstanding civic achievement. Despite these connections with the Garden Club of America, during the 1940s and 1950s Miss Hogg's primary attention turned away from the gardens at Bayou Bend. In part it started as a result of the war, but mainly it was caused by her involvement in other, very time-consuming activities. These pursuits included her new role in public service as a member of the Houston School Board, from 1943 to 1948. Also during the early 1940s, she purchased a few examples of American antique furniture, resuming a passion for Americana that had been her primary avocation in the period between 1920 and 1930. Around 1946 she began again to collect important museum-quality pieces, and by the 1950s she had become a major force on the national Americana-collecting scene. The increased

concentration in that area and her numerous acquisitions ultimately led her to decide to give her collection to the Museum of Fine Arts, Houston. By the mid-1950s, her thought process had moved toward leaving the collection in her home and to make Bayou Bend a house museum. The gift of Bayou Bend and the Bayou Bend Collection was made in 1957. It was also in the early 1950s that she began the restoration and historic furnishing of Varner Plantation, which was ultimately given to the Texas Department of Parks and Wildlife as a state park.

All these activities kept Miss Hogg from concentrating on her garden. Also, as she grew older, it became physically more difficult for her to give the gardens at Bayou Bend the detailed supervision she knew was required to maintain her standards of excellence. With characteristic vision and persuasiveness, she was able, in 1961, to arrange for River Oaks Garden Club to assume responsibility for overseeing the garden's management. This concept represented a parallel management role to that of the Museum of Fine Arts for the collection, although the ownership of the house and grounds was deeded to the museum along with the collection of Americana. Thus began a unique and successful relationship between the Garden Club and Bayou Bend that has flourished to the present day. In the summer of 1965, at the moment Miss Hogg was preparing to move from Bayou Bend to a new high-rise apartment, she took the time to express her satisfaction at how the Garden Club had assumed its role. Writing to the then-Garden Club chairman for Bayou Bend, she said, "It is comforting to know that you and your committee will be in charge of the gardens. . . . They certainly have improved the last three or four years under the management of the River Oaks Garden Club."[109]

After Miss Hogg moved away and Bayou Bend opened to the public, the role of the River Oaks Garden Club increased. Overall responsibility for the garden's administration was carried out by a Garden Club member appointed as chairman of the Bayou Bend Gardens. While there was a head gardener employed by the Garden Club and a staff of three other gardeners, Garden Club members themselves began to work in the garden from September through May, providing invaluable physical assistance in maintenance. In the mid-1960s it became policy for provisional members of the Garden Club to work in the gardens

Figure 61. The 'Duchesse de Caze' camellia.

Figure 60. 'Swiss Lake of Thun' pansies.

during their provisional year, and this practice has evolved into an important teaching and learning experience. At the suggestion of the author, then the new curator for the Bayou Bend Collection, the Garden Club also set up a committee to provide fresh, historically correct flower arrangements in the museum rooms of the house. These arrangements bring a continuing sense of life and freshness to the rooms of Miss Hogg's former home. In 1973, as virtually her last gift to Bayou Bend's gardens, Miss Hogg donated funds that enabled a greenhouse to be built at

Bayou Bend for the first time. As with the overall gardens, there has been a Garden Club chairman for the greenhouse and a team of volunteer workers. The greenhouse has become a valuable facility for the propagation for garden plants. In the 1990s, the Garden Club sought to reintroduce blue 'Lake of Thun' pansies at Bayou Bend (figure 60). Unable to find a reliable source, they eventually began to propagate them at Bayou Bend. Similarly the Garden Club and Bayou Bend's professional staff have begun a program to propagate rare old camellias, such as 'Duchesse de Caze,' which are today no longer available in the nurseries (figure 61). Over the years, Bayou Bend has emerged as an important part of River Oaks Garden Club's program for its members, and as an invaluable educational tool.

Following the Garden Club assuming responsibility for the gardens, Miss Hogg's own involvement did not cease. Rather, she maintained an intense interest in what she always referred to as "my garden." Though the major design and configuration of the gardens at Bayou Bend

Figure 62. The Carla Garden, c. 1975. *The Museum of Fine Arts, Houston, Archives.*

Americans in 1776, Miss Hogg suggested making topiaries of various animals representing the native fauna of the period. Located across the drive from the Butterfly Garden, the circular, brick-paved garden featured a parterre Texas star in the center, with topiary animals in five flanking segments: a deer, rabbit, squirrel, wild turkey and an American eagle. The garden, completed in the fall of 1976, was dedicated to Miss Hogg's memory (figure 63).[110]

In the mid-1960s, minor modifications were made to the gardens in anticipation of Bayou Bend becoming a house museum open to the public. First was the erection of a shelter for the security guard who would monitor traffic and greet guests arriving over a newly constructed footbridge spanning the bayou and connecting Bayou Bend with a parking lot on the other side.[111] Built as an octagonal cast-iron gazebo incorporating the same motifs found elsewhere on the house and gardener's cottage, the new guard structure was located at the center of the raised D-shaped brick terrace at the west end of the Clio Garden, earlier the site of the "Peach Garden" and the proposed "Green Garden." In another modification, the figure of Clio was rotated ninety degrees on its pedestal, so that arriving visitors would be presented with a profile, rather than back, view. Although this rotation interrupted the dialogue of more than a quarter century between the sculptures of two muses, Clio and Euterpe, which had been installed facing each other, Miss Hogg did not hesitate to have this change made, realizing that the first impression of visitors to her garden and collection superseded any sentimentality over past arrangements. Third, also to accommodate visitors, the narrow path of pink flagstone stepping-stones along the west side of the terraced lawn of the Diana Garden and by then the major visitor access to the house and collection of Americana, was replaced in 1968 with a wide, gracious brick walk. The new walk, which extended from the Clio Garden to the pink flagstone terrace on the north facade of the house, was designed by Pat Fleming. Fleming's design incorporated soft old antique brick, which linked it with the paving of the Clio Garden installed forty years earlier.

Miss Hogg modified plant material as well. For the East Garden, each year Miss Hogg searched for just the right blue 'Lake of Thun' pansies that were traditionally

today date from the golden era of the 1930s, there are two small gardens that were created in the 1960s and 1970s. First was the Carla Garden, named after Hurricane Carla, which in 1961 brought twisters that opened up a small area of woods directly south of Euterpe and below the East Garden. Miss Hogg decided to capitalize on what most people would have bemoaned as a disaster, and made a gravel-paved, circular area surrounded by azaleas in the hurricane-created glade. The design was refined in the early 1970s, and made both more permanent and more formal with the addition of brick paving to create a terrace edged with boxwood hedges and banked azaleas beyond (figure 62). The use of azaleas, boxwood, brick borders and paving tied the new design of the garden to the treatment used in the Clio Garden. The other garden, the last to be created at Bayou Bend, was conceived as a gift of River Oaks Garden Club in celebration of our nation's 1976 bicentennial. As the topiary was an important type of garden in the colonial period, the idea was to introduce it to Bayou Bend as a salute to the colonial era and a nod to the colonial Americana in the Bayou Bend Collection. However, as Texas was not yet settled by

Figure 63. The Topiary Garden.

Figure 64. Japanese magnolia.

planted in the lateral beds. However, voracious rabbits enjoyed a tradition of devouring these pansies. After Bayou Bend opened to the public, these beds became a prominent focal point for guests taking a break from the museum tour on the second-floor Glazed Porch overlooking the East Garden. Thus in 1966 she decided to replace the flowers planted there annually with Japanese boxwood planted in an ornamental scroll design reflecting that of the original wrought iron on the adjacent porch. Interestingly, Ruth London's June 1934 drawing (see figure 29) showed, as an alternate idea, boxwood planted in Greek key and scrolled designs in one of the lateral beds of what later was to become known as the East Garden.

Similarly, in the Clio Garden, the original roses did not do well and had been replaced with azaleas. The Kurume hybrid azaleas planted within the triangular boxwood parterres did not flourish after the weather became hot, which in Houston was a considerable portion of the year. As this garden was now the primary entry point for visitors to Bayou Bend, Miss Hogg, also in 1966, had the azaleas of the central section removed and replaced with small, dome-shaped, dwarf yaupon holly bushes.

Later in the 1960s, in an effort to extend the period of color in what had essentially been designed as a spring garden, Miss Hogg purchased a number of pink Japanese magnolias (figure 64), which bloomed in midwinter to early spring, and placed them on the eastern slope outside the Diana Garden room, adjacent to the woods. Not long after, in the early 1970s, she had pink crepe myrtle planted flanking the Diana reflecting pool at the edge of the woods, just outside the hedges on the north side of the Diana lawn (figure 65). Throughout the early to mid-summer, these hardy bushes, so popular in the antebellum garden, provide a wash of pink against the dark green of the woods behind them. Miss Hogg's final addition to the gardens at Bayou Bend was a modest memorial to her devoted gardener Alvin Wheeler, consisting of two small bronze sculptures of deer and a plaque, installed at the edge of the White Garden in 1971 (figure 66).

Over the years, other modifications were made within the gardens. One perennial problem since Miss Hogg's earliest days at Bayou Bend was erosion in the natural gullies and swales of the woodlands. Her simple approach had been both naturalistic and effective. She terraced the

Figure 65. Crepe myrtle.

banks of gullies near the Butterfly and East Gardens with stone and used ferns and monkey grass set out on the terraces to hold the soil. Erosion in the larger gullies between the Butterfly and White Gardens became progressively worse during the 1980s. Under the guidance of the Garden Club, Miss Hogg's technique was applied there as well, with great success. Small, stone-paved overlooks were placed intermittently along the edges, and today these tamed gullies provide a new visual accent within the

woodland garden (figure 67). Adjacent to one outlook, a collection of specimen ferns, a gift to Bayou Bend Gardens, was laid out on the slope leading down to the gully bottom. Similarly, a gift of specimen camellias was installed at the east end of the Butterfly Garden, at the edge of the woods.

Although these developments may appear to be major changes in the garden left by Miss Hogg, their impact was in fact minimal, as they lay outside what has become considered the historic areas of the garden. Indeed, remarkably, under the stewardship of River Oaks Garden Club for the last forty years, it has been possible to preserve and maintain the gardens with their original plant material and design. During the early period of the 1960s, when Bayou Bend first became a house museum, if not for River Oaks Garden Club's involvement and financial support, it is possible that changes or simplifications, in the name of efficiency and economy, might well have been implemented and that the 1930s golden-era historic gardens would have been lost. Fortunately, that did not happen to Bayou Bend, as it did to virtually all the other gardens in

Figure 66. A memorial to long-time Bayou Bend gardener Alvin Wheeler, installed near the White Garden.

Houston that were featured during the 1939 annual meeting of the Garden Club of America.

In 1967, to safeguard the future of Bayou Bend Gardens, River Oaks Garden Club, with generosity and vision, made an initial $10,000 gift to establish a permanent endowment to support the garden. Today the Bayou Bend Gardens Endowment has grown into a multimillion-dollar corpus, and the gardens have been both enriched and preserved over the years with its income. In another wise move, realizing that a garden evolves and changes over time, especially if there is no single person who has the collective memory and vision of that garden,

the Garden Club took steps to set up a committee to oversee proposed changes within Bayou Bend Gardens. That concept ultimately led to the realization that a master plan for the gardens was a requisite. Therefore, in 1993, Jon Emerson, historic landscape architect, was commissioned to draw up a master plan for Bayou Bend Gardens. A two-year study of the gardens themselves, review of archival records, and interviews with River Oaks Garden Club members active over the years ensued. In 1995, the resultant plan was adopted, and it has proven to be an important guideline toward both the choice of new plant material and returning the gardens to the look of their original design. One element of the plan established lists of plant material and color preferences documented as those chosen by Miss Hogg during her tenure at Bayou Bend. A second element called for restoration of gardens that had lost their original shape or look. These elements began to be implemented in stages. The first was restoration of the White Garden (figure 68). Formerly an open glade in the woods, the area had become so overgrown with large plant material that the sense of the original design was lost and the space had become claustrophobic. In clearing out the overgrowth, the original open design was recaptured; a brick-edged terraced progression into one of the adjacent swales, originally planted with various white plants like ginger lilies, was reclaimed. The second was an area between the drive and the woodland gardens to the east. Originally planted with camellias, spirea, and bulbs and left somewhat natural and a bit unkempt, over the years the area had been groomed and trimmed so that it lost its role as a screen between the White Garden beyond and the drive, and its naturalistic woodsy appearance had evolved into a sort of woodland lawn planted with English ivy. The ivy was removed and the natural undergrowth allowed to recapture the space. The third restoration, that of the Diana Garden, was the most extensive. Over the years, the azaleas in that garden had become oversized, blurring the crisp lines of Fleming and Sheppard's original design and burying the figure of Diana to her knees in foliage. Additionally the azaleas in front of Diana had been pruned into solid forms with hard contours, completely losing the natural, lacy contours that were an important part of the original composition. The arcing jets of water of the fountain had also lost their contour,

Figure 67. Erosion-controlled gullies in the woodland ravines.

and several of the ancient trees that framed the space had disappeared. New, appropriate azaleas were introduced, the fountain was repaired, and young trees were transplanted to conform with the original placement (figures 69 and 70). Additionally, a new gnarled oak was planted in the lower edge of the terraced steps, restoring that tension between the natural and the formal that was so characteristic of Miss Hogg's sensibilities. The result returned the garden to the design and spirit of its appearance on the momentous occasion in March 1939, nearly sixty years earlier, when it was unveiled to the ladies of the Garden Club of America.

Today, the importance of Miss Ima Hogg's garden at Bayou Bend can be viewed from several perspectives. First, it is an incredible resource for the residents of and visitors to Houston, a fourteen-acre oasis in the midst of urban sprawl. Open throughout the year to the public, with a variety of tours and programming, the gardens are an important horticultural and educational asset. Second,

Figure 68. The White Garden as it appears today.

Figure 69. The Diana Garden, prior to its restoration.

Figure 70. The Diana Garden, following its restoration to its original, more naturalistic state.

on a national level, Miss Hogg's creation at Bayou Bend represents an outstanding example of the neo-antebellum garden of the "Southern Garden Renaissance" and an extraordinarily well-preserved example of American gardening that accompanied the final stage of the Country House Movement. On a more local level, her garden stands as a monument to the golden age of gardening in Houston during the 1930s. Although a number of designers made contributions, it was Miss Ima Hogg's guiding spirit and sensibilities that give Bayou Bend's gardens their unique and personal character. Posterity is indeed fortunate to be able to enjoy the fruits of Miss Hogg's labors, her great southern garden, which she characterized as "a love affair with nature."

# Notes

1. Ima Hogg to William C. Hogg, telegram, April 5, 1929, Ima Hogg Papers, Center for American History, The University of Texas at Austin.

2. Ima Hogg, Introduction to *Bayou Bend Gardens* (Houston: privately printed for the Bayou Bend Gardens Endowment, 1975), n.p.

3. David F. Hood, "The Renaissance of Southern Gardens in the Early Twentieth Century," *Journal of Garden History* 16, no. 2 (April–June 1996): 129.

4. The fourth child, Thomas Elisha Hogg (1887–1949), who had become a resident of San Antonio by the time that Bayou Bend was built, was never involved with the house. Not atypical of the late nineteenth century, all of the family were known by nicknames: Jim and Sallie, Will, Mike, and Tom. As an adult, Ima was often called Miss Ima or Missima. Jim Hogg greatly admired an epic poem about the Civil War, *The Fate of Marvin,* written by his elder brother Thomas Elisha Hogg (1842–1880) and published in Houston in 1873. The heroine's name was Ima, a diminutive of the Scotch-Irish name Imogene. The poem describes her as a blue-eyed maid, a southern girl: "Ah she was fair; the Southern skies / were typed in Ima's heavenly eyes." Although the idea has been put forward that Jim Hogg was angry that the baby was not a son, in fact, three days after her birth, he wrote a glowing letter to another brother, John W. Hogg (1848–1912). "We have a daughter of as fine proportions and angelic mien as ever gracious nature favored a man with, and her name is Ima!" The Hoggs' first child, Ima's older brother Will, had been born nine years earlier. Thomas E. Hogg, *The Fate of Marvin* (Houston: E. H. Publisher, 1873), 9; Robert C. Cotner, *James Stephen Hogg, A Biography* (Austin: University of Texas Press, 1959), 89. The fiction that Ima had a twin sister named Ura dated from her father's political campaigns, when his opponents made the joke that there were two daughters.

5. Stinson, who had served as a colonel in the Confederate Army, remarried in 1866. His second wife, Mary A. Stinson (1836–1907), was the grandmother whose brick-bordered rose garden made an important impression on the young Ima, one she would recall vividly in later years. Ima Hogg, typescript manuscript of reminiscences dated 1973, Ima Hogg Papers.

6. Joseph Hogg's father, Thomas Blair Hogg (1768–1849), a planter in Georgia, became a major in the War of 1812, and in 1814 he entered the Georgia legislature. He moved west to Alabama in 1818 and entered that state's first legislature the next year. In 1831 he was a founder of the University of Alabama. In 1836 he moved again, to a large plantation at Bellefontaine, Mississippi. There, he was elected to the state legislature in 1839. Cotner, *James Stephen Hogg.*

7. In 1895, Jim Hogg set up housekeeping in a large house located at the corner of 19th and Rio Grande streets in Austin. That same summer, Sallie died of tuberculosis while on a health cure in Colorado.

8. Following Jim Hogg's death in 1906, Will Hogg became a business associate of Joseph S. Cullinan, Hogg's original partner in the Texas Company. In the summer of 1913, the New York-based directors of Texaco, as it was then called, wrested control of the company from the Texas directors and transferred the headquarters from Houston to New York. Hogg, who was secretary-treasurer, and Cullinan, who had been president of the company, immediately resigned and sold their stock. They established a new company, Farmers Petroleum, and would work together as partners until the relationship was broken off in 1919.

9. Interview, *Houston Post,* March 17, 1941.

10. Ima Hogg reminiscences, 1973, Ima Hogg Papers. The flower she recalls is very likely the orange-scarlet blossom of the fruiting pomegranate *(punica granatum).*

11. Ima Hogg, conversations with the author in the late 1960s. She later introduced the iris into her garden at Bayou Bend. Eventually, although Jim Hogg was working full-time in Houston as an attorney, he was shipping winter vegetables, English peas, and strawberries, from West Columbia to northern markets. Marguerite Johnston, *Houston, The Unknown City, 1836–1946* (College Station, Texas: Texas A&M University Press, 1991), 125.

12. Ima Hogg to Sarah Stinson Hogg, June 24, 1894, and June 26, 1894, Ima Hogg Papers. In 1898 Governor Hogg was invited to be a member of the United States delegation that was sent to Hawaii for the ceremonies surrounding the annexation of the kingdom as a United States territory. The sixteen-year-old Ima accompanied him. Her diary account of the trip strangely makes no comment on the lush, tropical flora, but she was curious to see the garden of Queen Liliuokalane at the Iolani Palace, and she and a friend managed to enter the grounds unobserved and wander about. Ima Hogg diary, 1898, Ima Hogg Papers.

13. These new Houston enclaves were typically characterized by a major landscaped street one or two blocks in length. The first, Westmoreland, was laid out in 1902, the year that Jim Hogg began to live in the Rice Hotel. Courtlandt Place was established in 1906, the year of Jim Hogg's death, and Montrose, where the Hogg children would move in 1917, was established in 1911. A fourth enclave, Shadyside, with which the Hogg children would have a lengthy but inconclusive involvement, was established in 1916.

14. In 1915, at the suggestion of Cullinan, the City of Houston retained Kessler to design a comprehensive landscape plan for Houston's parks, including the new Hermann Park. For further information on Kessler, see Charles A. Birnbaum and Robin Karson, eds., *Pioneers of American Landscape Design* (New York: McGraw Hill, 2000), 212–15.

15. For an illustration of the Shadyside plat and various lots, see Howard Barnstone, *The Architecture of John F. Staub: Houston and the South* (Austin: University of Texas Press, 1979), 6. Will Hogg memo to Cullinan, October 13, 1916, requesting he reserve a lot, and Cullinan's response, October 24, 1916, saying that he would reserve Lot Q. William C. Hogg Papers, Center for American History, The University of Texas at Austin.

16. Concurrently, the family's attention turned to improvements to the West Columbia plantation, by then called Varner Plantation. By this time, any ideas of living there full time had been abandoned, and Varner had become a weekend and vacation retreat. It is interesting to note the first phase of the project, begun in February 1916, was not work on the house, but improvements to the grounds, with the introduction of three magnolias and twenty satsumas. William C. Hogg diary, February 1916, William C. Hogg Papers. The Hoggs began to improve the grounds prior to consideration of the house, a pattern that was repeated at Bayou Bend a decade later. Birdsall Briscoe, a Houston architect who had attended the University of Texas with Will Hogg, was retained to design the remodeling, which was not realized until after World War I. Briscoe would later be a consulting architect for Bayou Bend.

17. Governor Sterling had built his own residence across the street. Other Rossmoyne neighbors included Frank Prior Sterling, Ross

Sterling's brother and a founder of Humble Oil, and Edgar Townes, chief legal counsel to Humble Oil. William S. Farish, another founder of Humble Oil, and his brother Stephen P. Farish lived one block away on Montrose Boulevard. Clearly the Hoggs' new residence was located in the midst of a fashionable area populated by the emerging elite of Houston's oil industry. The house was demolished in the 1960s. The street is today called Yoakum Boulevard.

18. At the end of the summer of 1918, Ima Hogg fell into a deep depression, a problem she would battle off and on for the rest of her life. By the late spring of 1919 she was sent by Will to Philadelphia, where she resided in the Main Line community of Merion during a "rest cure" treatment at Jefferson Medical College under the care of Dr. Francis X. Dercum, a noted neurologist. Although taking treatment, she was by no means confined, and she made frequent trips into New York City and spent the summers in Lake Placid. She returned to Houston in the spring of 1921. During a 1920 visit to New York, while posing for a portrait by Wayman Adams, she became curious about a colonial American maple chair in Adams's studio. Excited to learn that it was from the colonial period, Ima, who had not previously known that colonial furniture survived, shortly bought a very similar chair and thus began her famous collection of American furniture, a field which she continued to pursue for the next half century. Given in 1957 to the Museum of Fine Arts, Houston, the collection today is on view at Bayou Bend as the American decorative arts wing of the museum. See David B. Warren, Michael K. Brown, Elizabeth Ann Coleman, and Emily Ballew Neff, *American Decorative Arts and Paintings in the Bayou Bend Collection* (Princeton: Princeton University Press, 1998).

19. Hogg and Cullinan met in July 1919, shortly after Ima had entered treatment in Philadelphia. Hogg asked for a six-month extension of the option, which was refused. In September 1919 the lot was sold to William S. Farish. In October, Hogg withdrew from all his business relationships with Cullinan.

20. Home Improvements and Expenses at 4410 Rossmoyne Boulevard, William C. Hogg Papers.

21. At the time of his death in 1906, Jim Hogg had asked his children to retain Varner for a period of at least twenty years. He had noticed flammable gases in the marshy areas of the plantation and was sure that oil lay underneath. On January 15, 1918, the first successful well, Tyndall-Hogg number 2, came in, and the Hogg siblings, already wealthy, became fabulously rich.

22. Indeed, the Mount Vernon connection is made clear in a letter of Will Hogg, in which he wrote, "I tried to fix up the old place as George Washington would do if he had a bank roll." John Lomax, *Will Hogg, Texan* (Austin: University of Texas Press, 1956), 6.

23. The apartment was located in the newly fashionable area of apartment houses being built north of Grand Central Station after the New York Central tracks were covered over and Park Avenue created. The building, designed by Warren and Whetmore, actually had two addresses. The door to the south was numbered 280, the one to the north 290. Henry Francis du Pont, later a friend of Ima Hogg and a fellow collector of Americana, bought an apartment the previous year at 280 Park Avenue. At that time the two families were not acquainted. Ima was introduced to H. F. du Pont in the 1940s by his sister, Louise du Pont Crowninshield, with whom she had become friends when they both served on the board of the Garden Club of America. After

a 1954 visit to Bayou Bend, du Pont sent Miss Hogg eight cape jasmine bushes as a thank-you present. They were planted along the western edge of the drive adjacent to the Gardener's Cottage, but only lived for about twenty years. In the mid-1970s they were replaced with crepe myrtle.

24. Telegrams, Ima Hogg Papers. This was, of course, the same lot lost three years earlier when Joseph Cullinan would not extend Will Hogg's option. The Hogg siblings went so far as to review architectural drawings for a house being designed for Farish by New York architect Harry T. Lindeberg. When Farish eventually built the house, the work was supervised in Houston by Lindeberg's associate, John F. Staub, who would later design Bayou Bend.

25. The first, Colby Courts, was a small, twelve-acre tract on Main Street north of Shadyside. The initial plan was for Birdsall Briscoe, who was concurrently working on Varner, to lay out the enclave and design a house for the Hoggs. Realizing the tract was too small to ensure exclusivity and protection of the residents from the surrounding neighborhood, Hogg decided to develop it as an upper-middle-class neighborhood. The concepts of exclusivity and protection, and the need for adequate acreage to assure that, would be important factors in how River Oaks was later envisioned by Will Hogg. The second project, begun in partnership with Henry Stude, developed an area along White Oak Bayou that had formerly been the Stude farm. The project, called Norhill, was, like Colby Courts, not exclusive, but it did incorporate civic amenities, such as esplanade parks, which also presaged the design of River Oaks.

26. The interiors of the offices were in the Colonial Revival style. Ima took great interest in the details, making suggestions for the Greek Revival style framing of the French windows that gave access to the garden and advice on the proper white enamel paint for the woodwork and black for the colonial style hand-wrought door and window fixtures. This interest in the colonial and attention to detail anticipate what would evolve at Bayou Bend a few years later. The penthouse was furnished with Ima's colonial American furnishings, Windsor chairs, hooked rugs, Stiegel and Sandwich glass in the bookshelves as well as Will Hogg's collection of paintings by Frederic Remington. Indeed, in many ways creation of the Hogg Brothers' office served as an incubation stage for what Ima would create at Bayou Bend. See Emily Ballew Neff, *Frederic Remington: The Hogg Brothers Collection of the Museum of Fine Arts, Houston* (Princeton: Princeton University Press, 2000), 21–26.

27. Will Hogg offered to sell the property to the City of Houston at the same price he had paid for it, with the purchase payments spread over a period of ten years. He personally donated the first $50,000 toward the total cost and persuaded the adjacent land owner, the Reinerman Company, to sell the city an additional 630 acres at the same price, bringing the total acreage to 1,503.

28. In later years, Ima recalled encouraging her brother to think big, and indeed he did, eventually assembling 1,100 contiguous acres, as well as the Country Club Estates Company, and all the remaining unsold lots. Interview, November 8, 1974, with John F. Staub for Howard Barnstone's book on Staub, original tape now lost. See Barnstone, *John F. Staub*, xiv. The original Country Club Estates plat included streets with country club names extending several blocks east and west off the central boulevard. The 1,100-acre Hogg holdings extended from Shepherd Drive westward with the original 118 acres located roughly in the center.

29. For further information on Hare and Hare, see Birnbaum and Karson, *Pioneers of American Landscape Design,* 162–68.

30. The advantages to the Hogg real estate venture were manifold. When Buffalo Drive, as the new road was called, was finished, the River Oaks promotional literature boasted that the community was conveniently located just minutes by car from the center of Houston, closer to downtown than the new Museum of Fine Arts or Rice Institute. Clearly the Hoggs had learned a lesson from an earlier Houston suburb named Forest Hill, located in what should have been a highly desirable site, across Brays Bayou from the Houston Country Club. Laid out in 1910 by Hare and Hare and incorporating the first curvilinear streets for Houston, Forest Hills failed for the lack of good roads to the suburb. Cheryl Caldwell Ferguson, "River Oaks: 1920s Suburban Planning and Development in Houston," *Southwestern Historical Quarterly* (Texas State Historical Association) 104, no. 2 (October 2000), 196.

31. Included were Birdsall Briscoe, who had previously worked for the Hoggs at Varner, Sam H. Dixon, Jr., Joseph W. Northrup, and John F. Staub. Later, Charles Oliver was appointed permanent architect for the River Oaks Corporation, the name adopted for the Hoggs' company in 1927. For further discussion see ibid., 191–228.

32. The house did not sell immediately and eventually was purchased by the Hoggs' attorney, David Picton. Staub's second model house, in a more conservative Federal style was purchased by Country Club Estates' president, Hugh Potter. See Barnstone, *John F. Staub,* 77, 78, 81. In addition to the country club building, which was in the Spanish Colonial style, Staub was also retained to design the Baroque-style pink stucco gates to the community. Ima Hogg, who had been active in the selection of the other architects designing the model houses, took great interest in the outcome of their work. However, she was never as closely involved with those houses, ultimately nine in total, as she was on the pink stucco project with Staub.

33. The area was originally called "The Neighbors" and then "Contentment." The final name turned out to be "Homewoods," possibly in reference to Homewood, the historic Carroll family house in Baltimore, but more likely a simple play on words, referencing the naturally wooded nature of the site.

34. Will wrote from Houston to his sister, who was at 290 Park Avenue, about the proposed sizes of the lots: "Such points as this will be left in abeyance until you return and can be consulted and satisfied in every particular, for the 90 acres is going to be your own layout, if you will take responsibility of dictating the whole thing." October 12, 1925, William C. Hogg Papers. Joseph Cullinan had selected the largest site in Shadyside for his own home only ten years earlier. The effectiveness of that house as a draw could not have been lost on Will Hogg.

35. Ima Hogg to Julia Ideson, September 1925, Ima Hogg Papers. Julia Ideson (1880–1945), like Ima, attended the University of Texas, where she was a graduate of the first program in library science offered there. In 1903 she was appointed librarian of the new Houston Lyceum and Carnegie Library, a post she held for more than forty years. Houston's Spanish Colonial style Central Library building, erected in 1926, was later named for her.

36. Will Hogg to Ima Hogg, October 25, 1925, Ima Hogg Papers; Ima Hogg to Lyman Armes, April 30, 1927, William C. Hogg Papers.

37. Although today the house at Bayou Bend is customarily ascribed solely to Staub, all of the drawings for the house bear both their names as associate architects. The drawings are in the Bayou Bend Collection and Gardens Records, the Museum of Fine Arts, Houston, Archives. Each architect was paid an identical fee. William C. Hogg Papers. What apparently happened was the Hoggs' close friend Judge F. C. Proctor, who had purchased the Homewoods lot adjacent to Bayou Bend, wanted to build at the same time, so Staub and Briscoe divided the projects; Staub taking Bayou Bend, Briscoe the Proctor residence. Barnstone, *John F. Staub,* 107. See also note 54.

38. Ima Hogg to Marie (Mrs. Thomas E.) Hogg, February 8, 1926; Ima Hogg to Will Hogg, February 8, 1926; Ima Hogg to Dorothy (an unidentified friend), February 8, 1926, Ima Hogg Papers. Ima's youngest brother, Tom, had settled in San Antonio, where in 1923–24 he built a large Spanish Colonial style house in Olmas Park designed by prominent San Antonio architects Atlee and Robert B. Ayres. The house plans were published the year that Bayou Bend was completed; see *The American Architect* 134 (August 20, 1928): 237–39. At the same time as Ima's revealing letters, Will telegrammed her, "Don't hurry to choose house plans as Mickey [as Mike was called] and I want to collaborate, then too we want to know where you are going to get the money." Will Hogg to Ima Hogg, January 10, 1926, Ima Hogg Papers.

39. John Staub and his bride, Madeleine Delabarre Staub, spent their 1920 honeymoon in Charleston, where the young architect photographically documented the romantic old architecture of the city. Conversation of the author with their daughter, Caroline Staub Callery in the late 1990s. Undoubtedly these photographs served as sort of an incubator for ideas. Staub later laid out his ideas on New Orleans as a proper source of inspiration in a lucid article written in February 1928 for the Forum of Civics. He also discussed the use of pale apricot-pink stucco relieved by black ironwork and blue-green shutters, all details incorporated into his design for Bayou Bend. John F. Staub, "Latin Colonial Architecture in the Southwest," *Civics for Houston* 1, no. 2 (February 1928): 6–7. Staub wrote a similar article, "Latin Colonial Architecture," *Southern Architect and Building News* (August 1930): 32–35.

40. William C. Hogg diary, November 19, 1926, William C. Hogg Papers.

41. The thought process is revealed in a series of letters from Will Hogg to Staub and Briscoe. The first letter, after summarizing Hogg's view of the project, goes over the house plans point by point, with pithy critical comments. One complaint was that there were no dimensions given; another was that the change of level between the living room and library represented a safety hazard. Staub, feeling that a step down from the major drawing room to the library was a gracious feature, often incorporated changes in level in his plans. The one for Bayou Bend was eliminated. Hogg also requested that the stone terrace for the garden side be extended along the whole length of the house. Will Hogg to John Staub and Birdsall Briscoe, March 8 and 13, 1927, William C. Hogg Papers.

42. For a discussion of the house's design and Ima Hogg's recollections on the changed siting and the sacrifice of the porte cochère, see Barnstone, *John F. Staub,* 107–109.

43. Staub's letter of August 20, 1927, outlined his views on the cast iron-wrought iron question (Ima Hogg Papers). The cast iron—two different types of balustrade railing and a large amount of scroll borders that would be used on the two-story east terrace porch, a porch on the west end by the kitchen, and two smaller

porches on the south facade and on the east facade of the garage building—was ordered from the New Orleans firm Freitel Wrecking Company.

44. The material came from R. W. Burnham, a dealer in Ipswich, Massachusetts. Included was period paneling used in Miss Hogg's suite (today called the Queen Anne Bedroom and Sitting Room), beams and feather-edged sheathing used in the Tap Room (Murphy Room), and square bricks for the fireplaces in the Library (Pine Room), Blue Room (Massachusetts Room) and Miss Hogg's suite (Queen Anne Rooms). Undated Burnham Memorandum of Shipment, William C. Hogg Papers. Burnham also supplied new paneling and doors for the Blue Room. The old flooring had been intended for use in Miss Hogg's suite upstairs as well as in the Library, Blue Room, and Tap Room on the first floor, but when it arrived and was inspected, it turned out that much of it was in such bad condition as to be unusable. Ultimately, the period flooring was installed only in Miss Hogg's personal suite.

45. *Houston Post-Dispatch,* May 10, 1927, clipping, William C. Hogg Papers; *Houston Post-Dispatch,* August 26, 1928. In actuality, the cost came to $294,771.15, which included landscaping and a new Ford car for Mr. Staub; William C. Hogg Papers.

46. William C. Hogg diary, William C. Hogg Papers.

47. Will Hogg to Ima Hogg, telegram, January 10, 1926; Ima Hogg to Will Hogg, February 6, 1926; Bayou Bend Building records for March and April 1926 indicate that Teas Nursery and the Japanese Nursery Company supplied shrubs to Bayou Bend although the plant material is not identified. Ima Hogg Papers.

    In general, dogwood does not grow naturally or easily in Houston. At Bayou Bend, however, the deposits of sand from the occasional flooding of the bayou made the soil in the swales an ideal location for planting dogwood, and also for white oaks (which do not grow well elsewhere in Houston). The author is indebted to Bart Brechter, curator of gardens at Bayou Bend, for this information.

48. The source was one of Houston's most prominent nineteenth-century gardens, which filled the entire block of Louisiana Avenue between McKinney and Lamar streets, and surrounded the residence of Thomas W. House, Jr. The magnolia, an important feature of the garden, had been planted about the time the residence was built in 1872. Moving the 25,000-pound tree, done under the supervision of Worthington E. Davey, was of sufficient interest to be recounted in an article in the April 3, 1926 issue of the *Houston Chronicle.* Where the tree was planted at Bayou Bend and its ultimate fate remain a mystery. The House family were close friends of the Hoggs. Thomas's brother Edward House, who managed Jim Hogg's gubernatorial campaigns and later became a close adviser to Woodrow Wilson, accompanied Ima on her trip to Egypt in February 1926.

49. The company principal, Conway Blume, a native of Louisiana, had studied horticulture in California with Luther Burbank. Blume report, Ima Hogg Papers.

50. The scheme of steps progressing on axis down the hill to a focal point echoes ideas sketched four years earlier by Will Hogg in a design for a 129-acre property west of Houston at the intersection of Westheimer and Kuykendahl roads, which he called "My Country Place." In that sketch, a grape arbor extends on axis from the house to a large swimming pool of approximately 25 by 70 feet. William C. Hogg Papers. The Hare and Hare drawing is in the Ima Hogg Papers.

51. Two years earlier Ima had written a friend, "I think the house is going to be lovely. My own thought is that it isn't going to be too big, though it is considerably cut down since I showed the plans to you." Ima Hogg to Dorothy (an unidentified friend), February 8, 1926, Ima Hogg Papers.

52. The August 1928 date is important because the *Houston Post-Dispatch* photograph clearly shows the sloping hill cleared of underbrush and belies the later lore, as told to the author by landscape architect Pat Fleming, that, prior to 1937, the north side of the house was a thicket of woods coming right up to the terrace. See David B. Warren, "Bayou Bend: The Plan and History of the Gardens," *The Museum of Fine Arts, Houston, Bulletin* 12, no. 2 (winter-spring 1989): 72–77. H. E. Brigham, letter indicating Miss Hogg was not ready to interview gardeners, November 21, 1928, Ima Hogg Papers.

53. Bayou Bend Collection and Gardens Records.

54. Drawing, Ima Hogg Papers. At the same time, the Hoggs were interacting with Caldwell on other fronts: Will suggested that he and his sister be consulted for a "Magnolia Walk" for River Oaks (Will Hogg memorandum to Hugh Potter, December 14, 1928, Ima Hogg Papers); and Caldwell contributed an article to the December 1928 issue of "Civics for Houston," a magazine that Will Hogg published to promote urban planning and design. Caldwell was also the designer of the garden next door to Bayou Bend at the home of Judge Proctor, which was being built simultaneously with Bayou Bend. For discussion of that house, later the home of Mike Hogg, and attribution of the garden design to Caldwell, see *Garden Club of America Annual Meeting 1939,* a nonpaginated commemorative book published in conjunction with the Annual Meeting in Houston, February/March 1939.

55. The general layout of the Caldwell plan relates closely to one that appeared in a then-current gardening book, Louisa Yeomans (Mrs. Francis) King, *Variety in the Little Garden* (Boston: The Atlantic Monthly Press, 1923), 56–57. This book appears in a 1933 inventory of books owned by Miss Hogg, although when she acquired it is not known. Mrs. King was a leading figure in the garden club movement and a founder of the Garden Club of America. Birnbaum and Karson, *Pioneers of American Landscape Design,* 216–17.

56. During the antebellum period, Americans in the Deep South with new wealth from agricultural crops began to build expensive homes; they also surrounded them with elaborate gardens. Almost invariably these gardens, which were intended to serve as an indication of the taste and social prestige of the newly wealthy owners, were of conservative, formal design incorporating geometric principals that had characterized gardens of the colonial era in Virginia and South Carolina. For further discussion, see James R. Cothran, *Gardens and Historical Plants of the Antebellum South* (Columbia, South Carolina: University of South Carolina Press, 2003), 9 ff. This type of garden, although *retardataire,* nonetheless became the archetypical antebellum model that was later emulated during the "Southern Garden Renaissance" of the early twentieth century.

57. Household disbursements for April 1929 indicate that Houston House Wrecking Company supplied 3,400 old bricks. The River Oaks Corporation, according to a November 21, 1929, memo to Will Hogg summarizing expenses at Bayou Bend, supplied lumber for the walk forms for the "rose garden." Ima Hogg Papers.

58. *Houston Chronicle,* April 5–8, 1929; *Houston Post-Dispatch,* April 6–9, 1929; *Houston Press,* April 16–18, 1929. By May, head gardener George Fitch and gardeners Kyle Sims and James Wall had been hired. Alvin Wheeler, Miss Hogg's beloved long-time gardener, was not hired until the fall of 1930. The evidence of Caldwell's design for the upper garden, and Wheeler's arrival at Bayou Bend a year and one half after the creation of the lower garden, make it clear that the 1970s oral tradition that Wheeler and Ima Hogg laid out the designs of these two gardens is not true. A photograph of "roses in a corner of Miss Ima Hogg's garden" was published in the *Houston Chronicle,* April 19, 1931.

59. H. E. Brigham, manager of Hogg Brothers, to Ima Hogg, June 4, 1930, with an enclosure summarizing bills from Teas Nursery dating November 15–March 29, 1930, Ima Hogg Papers. Ima Hogg's views on the transplanting of dogwood were shared with the author during a conversation in the late 1960s.

60. Teas Nursery supplied 24 Cecile Brunner, 30 Kaiserin Auguste Viktoria, 26 Lady Hillingdon, 88 dwarf pink baby ramblers, and 32 Red Radiance tree roses in March. The old-time and tree roses were acquired from E. A. McIlhenny of Avery Island, Louisiana, who ran a large nursery business called "Jungle Gardens." A few years later, Miss Hogg would begin to purchase important azaleas and camellias from him.

61. The amount of the fee corresponds almost identically to a fee of $65 paid to Houston Studio Gardens by Miss Hogg's brother, Mike Hogg, for a garden plan made by Ruth London for his house next door to Bayou Bend (statement of expenses at 2950 Lazy Lane, May 2, 1932, Mike and Alice Hogg Papers, the Museum of Fine Arts, Houston, Archives; London payment, household accounts, Ima Hogg Papers). Houston Studio Gardens was founded in 1929 by Mrs. Walter B. Sharp. With her partner, Vera Baker Chinn, she first ran the business from 4410 Rossmoyne Boulevard, which she had purchased from the Hoggs in 1928. Chinn was a graduate of the Lowthorpe School of Landscape Architecture and Horticulture for Women in Groton, Massachusetts. The school was founded 1901 by Mrs. Julia Motley Low to provide the opportunity for women to study landscape architecture denied them at Harvard, at that time the major place for study in the field. All students and faculty were women. In late 1929 or early 1930, Mrs. Sharp hired Pennsylvania native Ruth London as the firm's landscape designer. London, a 1928 Lowthorpe graduate, had apprenticed in New York with landscape architects Agnes Selkirk and Isabella Pendleton prior to coming to Houston. Another New York City landscape architect, Ellen Biddle Shipman, who later became involved with Bayou Bend, taught at Lowthorpe.

62. Drawings and household account payments to J. L. Hoffman for drayage on fifty wild peaches, two hundred fifty azaleas, and forty-one dogwood, December 1931, Ima Hogg Papers.

63. The concept of a "green garden" was discussed in Forum of Civics, *A Garden Book for Houston* (Houston: Forum of Civics, 1929), 88. A green garden is ". . . without color other than that of the foliage. Such a garden suggests restfulness and quiet, even under the glaring sun."

64. On the possible location of the Green Garden at the east end of the house, see Sally Robert Banttari, "The Evolution of the Bayou Bend Gardens, Houston, Texas (1926–1989)" (master's thesis, Louisiana State University, 1989), 113–16; Kelly McCaughey Allegrezza, "Ruth London (1893–1966): Houston Landscape Architect" (master's thesis, Louisiana State University, 1999), 63–64.

65. Miss Hogg was typically away for the summer, that year in New Mexico. The hurricane damage was described to her in detail by the Hogg Brothers manager, Mr. H. E. Brigham. Brigham to Ima Hogg, August 23 and September 2, 1932, Ima Hogg Papers. Miss Hogg spent the summer of 1933 at the Mayo Clinic in Rochester, Minnesota. In the fall she went to Tucson, where she remained under treatment at the Wyatt Clinic until February 1934.

66. These were supplied by Teas Nursery; household accounts, March 1930, Ima Hogg Papers.

67. Miss Hogg's garden notebook for the spring of 1933 records planting new camellias around the azalea garden. Bayou Bend Collection and Gardens Records. The next entry is Ruth London's "Design Plan of Azalea Garden of Miss Ima Hogg . . ." dated July 26, 1934. Ima Hogg Papers.

68. H. Harold Hume, *Azaleas and Camellias* (New York: Macmillan, 1931). In the back of Miss Hogg's copy, now in the Bayou Bend library, she wrote out extensive notes "for planting" and also "for fertilizing," clearly indicating her mastery of conditioning and maintaining the soil for azaleas: "For planting / 4 wheel barrows turf loam (leaf) / 2 ditto granulated peat moss / 1 ditto good sharp sand / 1 gal sulfaphosphate (acid base) / 1½ ditto cotton seed meal / ½ ditto aluminum sulphate. Place in deep hole before setting azalea. Fertilizing azaleas 1 years planting or more / Aluminum sulphate / Cotton Seed Meal / Scratch around azalea plant not more than ½ inch deep and sprinkle a large handful on the ground and rake it gently." Her notation about Bellingrath Gardens refers to those famed azalea gardens in Mobile, Alabama, which opened to the public that same year, 1932.

69. The first mention of camellias occurs in the March and April 1932 household accounts which list expenses for camellia trees that Ima and Mike Hogg purchased in Louisiana from Clovis Chargois; Ima Hogg Papers. While the identity of Chargois is unknown, Miss Hogg would again turn to him as a source of camellias for the East Garden in 1935. The second group was purchased from E. A. McIlhenny of Avery Island; Garden notebook, Bayou Bend Collection and Gardens Records. By 1934, McIlhenny, who was selling not only to Miss Hogg but also to other Houston gardeners, opened a Houston subsidiary, a depot named Jungle Gardens at the northeast corner of River Oaks Boulevard and Westheimer Road, where it remained until after World War II. Mrs. Arthur Boice, formerly the horticulturist at Houston Studio Gardens, was McIlhenny's manager in Houston.

70. Brigham's comments were quoted to Miss Hogg in an October 13, 1933, letter from Herbert Kipp; her queries to Mr. Brigham in an undated letter and in another dated November 4, 1933, Ima Hogg Papers.

71. Ima Hogg to H. E. Brigham, September 4, 1934, Ima Hogg Papers. "OK" was one of the Bayou Bend gardeners.

72. Earlier I had suggested that the sketch was Ellen Biddle Shipman's; Warren, "Bayou Bend: The Plan and History of the Gardens," 70. In actuality, Shipman only first visited Houston in March 1935, by which time this garden was well under way. Additionally the handwriting, when compared with other samples such as that on the Peach Garden drawing, is clearly Ruth London's, and the later 1934 drawing by London confirms her authorship of the design for this garden.

73. Ima Hogg Papers.

74. Interestingly, in 1966, clipped boxwood scrolls were introduced into the East Garden's lateral beds.

75. This scheme had precedent in a garden room designed by London in 1933 for Mr. and Mrs. Robert Weir's residence on North Boulevard, which featured azaleas ranging in color from salmon through apple blossom placed against a yaupon hedge. *Garden Club of America Annual Meeting 1939* booklet, n.p., Bayou Bend Collection and Gardens Records. The camellias originally were Duchesse de Caze.

76. For camellias, Miss Hogg once again turned in September to Clovis Chargois in Louisiana who held eighteen trees for her until she could see them in bloom, and also to E. A. McIlhenny two months later. McIlhenny also supplied a large number of azaleas. Other azaleas were supplied by T. Kiyono of Mobile. H. E. Brigham to Ima Hogg, September 19, 1934; Bayou Bend household payments, November 1934, $235 to McIlhenny, and December 1934, $247 to Kiyono; Ima Hogg Papers.

77. Hinderer's Iron Works to Ruth London, April 19, 1934, Ima Hogg Papers; Hinderer's catalogue, Bayou Bend Collection and Gardens Records. The lyre-decorated ironwork gates are very similar in design to a pair of gates supplied at the same time by Berger Ornamental Iron Works in Houston. A letter from Berger quoting the price to Miss Hogg notes that they were designed by Houston Studio Gardens, i.e., Ruth London. Those gates are today at the north and south sides of the D-shaped terrace on the site of the former Peach Garden; Berger to Ima Hogg, April 3, 1935. The drawing for those gates also survives; Ima Hogg Papers. The lyre-back chairs and settees made by Houston's Weber Iron Works, still today in use throughout the gardens at Bayou Bend, were acquired in the spring of 1936; household payments to Weber, April 1936, $534 with the notation "metal chairs," and May 1936, $298.75; Ima Hogg Papers.

78. Garden Book, Bayou Bend Collection and Gardens Records; Dogwood purchase from E. H. West, household accounts, March 1935, Ima Hogg Papers; discussion of White Garden, in section titled "Special Gardens," Forum of Civics, *Garden Book for Houston,* 87.

79. *Houston Post,* March 22, 1936. The briefer account of the White Garden is from Mrs. Allan Hannay, *Houston Magazine,* April 1936. On March 22, 1936, Bayou Bend and two other houses, the Mike Hogg and Harry Hanszen residences, also on Lazy Lane, were opened for a special two-day pilgrimage that preceded the annual Azalea Trail that was sponsored by the River Oaks Garden Club and held in April. The first Azalea Trail took place only two years earlier, when twelve River Oaks gardens were opened in late April at a cost of 25 cents each.

80. Sources were Overlook Nurseries in Crichton, Alabama; Longview Camellia Specialist, with locations in Crichton and Mobile; and Coolidge Rare Plant Gardens, Ltd., in Pasadena, California. Varieties mentioned included: Madonna, Lady Vanity, Duke d'Orleans, and Opelousa Pink from Overlook; and Purity, Valvareda, Cheerful, Aloha, Donklaeri, and Rainy Sun from Coolidge. List from Overlook, January 21, 1937; invoice from Coolidge, February 2, 1937, Bayou Bend Collection and Gardens Records.

81. McIlhenny to Ima Hogg, January 27, 1937, and December 1, 1937, Ima Hogg Papers. A January 1937 list of grafted camellias from McIlhenny included one each of Mathotiana rubra, Mototiana rosa, Tokayama, Adolphe Adusson Orinono-nishiku, noted as "new white," Minenoyuke, also noted as white, and lastly twenty of the camellias he was developing for her, Missima. The second order of eight prize grafts, followed by descriptions as given in McIlhenny's 1937 plant list, were: Paulina ("large double rich"); Alizarin ("crimson white blotched"); Laurel Leaf ("double solid clear pink"); Lelia ("double shell pink"); Kellingtonia ("very large peony bright deep red blotched white"); Magniflora ("semi double delicate flesh pink"); Purple Dawn ("perfect double deep red, purple"); and Red Ball ("very large full peony deep red"). "A List with Short Descriptions of More Than 600 Varieties of Camellias in the Home Grounds (Jungle Gardens) of E. A. McIlhenny" (Avery Island, Louisiana: 1937). The January 1937 list and Miss Hogg's personal copy of McIlhenny publication are in the Bayou Bend Collection and Gardens Records. The latter bears her customary check marks next to the names of the camellias that interested her.

82. Examples include an extensive new camellia garden designed by Ellen Biddle Shipman for Mrs. John E. Green at 2970 Lazy Lane; an entirely new garden, also designed by Shipman for Mrs. Richard W. Neff at 1506 South Boulevard; new gardens designed by Fleming and Sheppard for Mrs. George Heyer at 2909 Inwood Drive, and Mrs. Ray Dudley at 3371 Chevy Chase Drive. Ruth London also worked on the Dudley garden. Each of these gardens was on the itinerary for the 1939 meeting.

83. Warren, "Bayou Bend: The Plan and History of the Gardens," 77.

84. That this phase of the work was completed by June 1937 is confirmed by payments made then to the landscape contractor, Tom Harwood, and the builder, Chris Miller, who raised the wall; to Tom Harwood of Houston Lawn Service for "planting terrace," $535; to Chris Miller, $345; June 1937, household accounts, Ima Hogg Papers.

85. Ima Hogg to H. E. Brigham, June 4, 1937; Brigham to Hogg, June 22, 1937; Hogg to Brigham, July 6, 1937, Ima Hogg Papers.

86. Antonio Frilli to Ima Hogg, July 21, 1937; Frilli to Hogg, August 7, 1937; undated reply, Hogg to Frilli, asking for the price in dollars, and a second undated reply offering to round Frilli's payment to $1,150; Bayou Bend Collection and Gardens Records.

87. Marino Baroni to Ima Hogg, July 17 and July 27, 1937, Bayou Bend Collection and Gardens Records; Ima Hogg to H. E. Brigham, n.d.; household accounts, September 27, 1937, Ima Hogg Papers.

88. The Diana of Versailles, an antique Roman sculpture, was given by Pope Paul IV to the French king, Henry II, in 1556. The statue was first placed in the garden at Fontainebleau, and in 1602 it was transferred to the Louvre. During the reign of Louis XIV it was placed in the Grand Gallery at Versailles, and in 1798 it was returned to the Department of Antiquities at the Louvre, where it remains today.

89. Mac Griswold and Eleanor Weller, *The Golden Age of American Gardens: Proud Owners, Private Estates, 1890–1930* (New York: Harry N. Abrams, 1991), 229. Weeks Hall created a neo-antebellum garden at Shadows on the Teche in the 1930s and introduced classical figures there at that time; ibid., 233. There is, however, no information that Ima Hogg knew Hall or ever visited Shadows on the Teche.

90. Barnstone, *John F. Staub,* 178; for a discussion of the Cullen garden, see *Garden Club of America Annual Meeting 1939* booklet, n.p.; mention of the new statues for the Greens' garden appeared in the April 19, 1935, issue of the *Houston Press.* A much earlier instance of classically inspired garden statuary in Houston was found in the garden surrounding a colonial-revival style house built in 1910 on McGowan Avenue by Robert Duff. That garden featured life-sized stone figures of Venus, Psyche, and a faun. Dorothy Knox Howe Houghton, Barrie Scardino, Sadie Gwin

Blackburn, and Katherine S. Howe, *Houston's Forgotten Heritage: Landscape, Houses, Interiors, 1824–1914* (Houston: Rice University Press, 1991), 177–78. Although there is no evidence that Miss Hogg knew the Duffs, Houston was a very small community at that time, and there is every possibility that she was aware of that garden as well.

91.  From the accounts of expenses at the Mike Hogg garden, cited above, we know that London charged $5 an hour. At that rate, she then provided Miss Hogg with twelve hours' service prior to June. That London's involvement at Bayou Bend after that time was minimal is confirmed by the small amounts paid her subsequently; December 1937, $6.25; January 1938, $17.00; and finally February 1938, $17.84; household accounts, Ima Hogg Papers.

92.  Ima Hogg to Antonio Frilli, November 15, 1937; Frilli to Hogg November 25, 1937; Bayou Bend Collection and Gardens Records. Frilli noted that the shipment was being handled by his agent Zanes.

93.  Daily Reminder, 1938; diary, 1938; household accounts personal checkbook, February 12, 1938; Ima Hogg Papers. Shipman's brochure indicated that she was available for consultation on small gardens at $25, and at $50 to $100 for larger places. The payment of $106 probably included incidental expenses for which she charged above and beyond the consultation fee.

94.  Interview, May 27, 1987; for the article based on that interview, see Warren, "Bayou Bend: The Plan and History of the Gardens," 77–79.

95.  Albert Sheppard, handwritten notes of April 1997 on a letter from David B. Warren to Albert Sheppard, August 30, 1996, Bayou Bend Collection and Gardens Records.

96.  "Flower Lovers to Hear Mrs. Shipman March 25. Decidedly the most important gardening event of the year in Houston will be the lecture by Mrs. Ellen Biddle Shipman, dean of American women landscape architects . . ." *Houston Press,* March 1, 1935. The item about the Shipman's consultation with Miss Hogg appeared in *Houston Press,* January 19, 1938.

97.  In 1935 the Garden Club of America made a visit to Japan. As part of that visit they published a book illustrating members' gardens as a presentation gift to their hosts in Japan. A copy of that book, now in the library of the MFAH bears the book plate of Estelle B. Sharp, Miss Hogg's close friend and founder of Houston Studio Gardens. As other Houstonians probably had copies of the book, it is difficult to believe that Miss Hogg had not seen it. The Bulkley garden is illustrated as plate 1. Garden Club of America, *Gardens of America* (privately printed by the Garden Club of America, 1935). See also Judith Tankard, *The Gardens of Ellen Biddle Shipman* (Sagaponack, New York: Sagapress, Inc., 1996), 146.

98.  Ima Hogg diary, 1908, Ima Hogg Papers. In an interview on May 28, 1998, Mrs. Streeter, the granddaughter of Ellen Shipman, brought the analogy of the Duke Gardens to Bayou Bend to the author's attention. For discussion of the Sarah P. Duke Garden in Durham, North Carolina, see Tankard, *Ellen Biddle Shipman,* 170–74.

99.  More than eight hundred drawings for some ninety projects were donated by Pat Fleming to the Houston Metropolitan Research Center of the Houston Public Library in the early 1990s. By that time, any drawings that Fleming had for Bayou Bend had been separated from the main body and were subsequently lost. The surviving replica was made for Banttari, "The Evolution of the Bayou Bend Gardens."

100. Albert Sheppard, interview with the author, August 23, 1996.

101. Ima Hogg to E. A. McIlhenny, telegrams, November 5 and 9, 1938; McIlhenny response, November 8, 1938; Hogg to McIlhenny, November 12, 1938; McIlhenny to Hogg, November 15, 1938; Ima Hogg Papers. Early photos show that the green marble base was initially used; it is unknown when it was replaced with the simple brick pedestal there today.

102. Ima Hogg to E. A. McIlhenny, May 27, 1983, Avery Island Archives, Avery Island, Louisiana.

103. Ima Hogg to Antonio Frilli, telegram, October 30, 1938; Frilli to Hogg, November 1 and 5, 1938; Bayou Bend Collection and Gardens Records.

104. Antonio Frilli to Ima Hogg, February 11, 1938; Bayou Bend Collection and Gardens Records.

105. The Shadyside house of Mrs. Harry C. Wiess located at the corner of Main Street and Sunset Boulevard had been designed by William Ward Watkin and altered by Harry Lindeberg. The gardens were designed by Ruth London and Ellen Biddle Shipman.

106. Program notes, *Garden Club of America Annual Meeting 1939,* Bayou Bend Collection and Gardens Records.

107. Albert Sheppard, interview with the author, August 23, 1996. For Fleming's fantasy description of the Butterfly Garden's creation, see Warren, "Bayou Bend: The Plan and History of the Gardens," 87.

108. The garden was featured in the *Houston Chronicle,* March 1, 1942, which provided the description of the various flowers and the "Chinese grass." This is likely what is known today as mondo grass or monkey grass, a plant that actually originated in Japan.

109. Ima Hogg to Mrs. Gail Borden Tennant, July 7, 1965, Bayou Bend Collection and Gardens Records.

110. The revised Carla Garden was designed by Janet Wagner, and the Topiary Garden was designed by Gregory Catlow, both landscape architects based in Houston. Unfortunately, the type of topiary installed, fig ivy growing over wire armatures, never flourished and suffered especially from the periodic freezing weather of Houston's winters. The result was that the garden did not meet the high standards held elsewhere in the Bayou Bend Gardens. Therefore, in 2003 the River Oaks Garden Club, following Miss Hogg's own precepts of recognizing a problem and then taking steps to create a better situation, removed the wire-armature topiary figures and appointed a committee to study a solution to the creation of new ones. At the time of writing the solution had not been finalized.

111. After Miss Hogg announced her intention of giving Bayou Bend to the Museum of Fine Arts, Houston, to be a decorative arts museum, citizens of River Oaks threatened a lawsuit to prevent the visiting public from driving through the private enclave. A solution was found when land across the Buffalo Bayou immediately west of Bayou Bend, originally a separate parcel of the Memorial Park transaction, was developed by the City of Houston to provide access to Bayou Bend and a parking lot outside of River Oaks.

# A PORTRAIT OF
# BAYOU BEND GARDENS

The driveway approaching Bayou Bend

Aerial view of Bayou Bend from the southeast

*Opposite and above:* The south facade

*Opposite and above:* The north facade

View from the central hall of the house onto
the Diana Garden

View of the Diana Garden

*Left and above:* Steps on the Diana Lawn

An urn on the Diana Lawn wall

*Opposite and above:* The Diana Fountain

The figure of Diana

Crepe myrtle in the Diana Garden

The Diana Garden

Azaleas in bloom

Tulips and azaleas

Redbud tree

*Above and below:* Sculpture of Clio

*Opposite:* The Clio Garden

*Above and opposite:* Gate in the Clio Garden

Lead figures of children in the East Garden

The East Garden

93

A majestic sycamore tree near the Euterpe Garden

The East Garden

The Euterpe Garden

Tulips and azaleas

Dogwoods and azaleas

Loblolly pine and southern magnolia trees on
the lawn near the Butterfly Garden

The Butterfly Garden

Lead figure of Cupid in the Butterfly Garden

The Butterfly Garden

Azaleas in bloom

Tulips and azaleas

*Left and below:* The White Garden

Dogwoods

Dogwood blossom

*Above:* Azaleas in bloom

*Below left:* Daffodils

*Below right:* 'George Lindsey Tabor' azalea

Towering pines

Crepe myrtle
blooming in the
woods

Azaleas along a woodland path

*Above and opposite page:* Wooded ravines

Azaleas and dogwood,
with Japanese magnolia
in the background

*Opposite page and above:* Wooded ravines

The Buffalo Bayou bends around the property

Lush vegetation along the banks of a ravine

Steps along a wooded path

The Diana Fountain at night

# APPENDIX  Plants in Bayou Bend Gardens Today

BY BART BRECHTER, *Curator, Bayou Bend Gardens*

| Botanical Name | Hybrid/Cultivar | Common Name | Origin |
|---|---|---|---|
| *Abelia x grandiflora* | | Glossy abelia | China |
| *Acanthus mollis* | | Acanthus, bear's breech | Southern Europe |
| *Acer rubrum var. 'Drummondii'* | | Drummond red maple | United States (Texas) |
| *Adiantum capillus-veneris* | Southern maidenhair | Southern fern | United States |
| *Ajuga reptans* | 'Alba' | White ajuga | Europe |
| *Ajuga reptans* | | Bugleweed | Europe |
| *Ardesia crenata* | | Christmas berry | China |
| *Aspidistra elatior* | | Apidistra, cast iron plant | Japan |
| *Aspidistra elatior* | 'Milky Way' | Milky Way aspidistra | Japan |
| *Aspidistra elatior* | 'Variegata' | Variegated aspidistra | China |
| *Asplenium bulbiferum* | | Mother fern | |
| *Asplenium platyneuron* | | Ebony spleenwork fern | United States |
| *Athyrium filix* | | Lady fern | United States |
| *Athyrium goeringianum* | 'Pictum' | Japanese painted fern | Japan |
| *Begonia coccinea* | | Angel wing begonia | Brazil |
| *Bletilla striata 'alba'* | | White ground orchid | Japan, China |
| *Buxus microphylla var. japonica* | | Japanese boxwood | Japan |
| *Callacarpa americana var. alba* | | Beautyberry | United States (Texas) |
| *Camellia hiemalis* | 'Shishi-gashira' | Camellia hiemalis | Japan |
| *Camellia japonica* | 'Rev. John G. Drayton' | Camellia | Japan |
| *Camellia japonica* | 'Adolphe Audusson' | Camellia | Japan |
| *Camellia japonica* | 'Alba Plena' | Camellia | Japan |
| *Camellia japonica* | 'Boule de Neige' | Camellia | Japan |
| *Camellia japonica* | 'Brilliant' | Camellia | Japan |
| *Camellia japonica* | 'Coronation' | Camellia | Japan |
| *Camellia japonica* | 'Debutante' | Camellia | Japan |
| *Camellia japonica* | 'Dr. Tinsley' | Camellia | Japan |
| *Camellia japonica* | 'Drama Girl' | Camellia | Japan |
| *Camellia japonica* | 'Duchesse de Caze' | Camellia | Japan |
| *Camellia japonica* | 'Duchesse de Caze Pink' | Camellia | Japan |
| *Camellia japonica* | 'Elisabeth' | Camellia | Japan |
| *Camellia japonica* | 'Fanny Boils' | Camellia | Japan |
| *Camellia japonica* | 'Gloire de Nantes' | Camellia | Japan |
| *Camellia japonica* | 'Herme' | Camellia | Japan |

| Botanical Name | Hybrid/Cultivar | Common Name | Origin |
|---|---|---|---|
| Camellia japonica | 'Jarvis Red' | Camellia | Japan |
| Camellia japonica | 'La Peppermint' | Camellia | Japan |
| Camellia japonica | 'Lady Clare' | Camellia | Japan |
| Camellia japonica | 'Lady Vansittart' | Camellia | Japan |
| Camellia japonica | 'Leucantha' | Camellia | Japan |
| Camellia japonica | 'Mathotiana' | Camellia | Japan |
| Camellia japonica | 'Mme. Cachet' | Camellia | Japan |
| Camellia japonica | 'Otome' | Camellia | Japan |
| Camellia japonica | 'Pink Perfection' | Camellia | Japan |
| Camellia japonica | 'R. L. Wheeler' | Camellia | Japan |
| Camellia japonica | 'Rose Dawn' | Camellia | Japan |
| Camellia japonica | 'Rutledge Minnix' | Camellia | Japan |
| Camellia japonica | 'Sarah Frost' | Camellia | Japan |
| Camellia japonica | 'Wildwood' | Camellia | Japan |
| Camellia japonica | 'Winifred Womak' | Camellia | Japan |
| Camellia sasanqua | 'Apple Blossom' | Camellia sasanqua | Japan |
| Camellia sasanqua | 'Cotton Candy' | Camellia sasanqua | Japan |
| Camellia sasanqua | 'Day Dream' | Camellia sasanqua | Japan |
| Camellia sasanqua | 'Lesliann' | Camellia sasanqua | Japan |
| Camellia sasanqua | 'Maiden's Blush' | Camellia sasanqua | Japan |
| Camellia sasanqua | 'Mine-no-yuki' | Camellia sasanqua | Japan |
| Camellia sasanqua | 'Pink Snow' | Camellia sasanqua | Japan |
| Camellia x hybrid | 'Fragrant Pink' | Camellia non-reticulata hybrid | Japan |
| Carpinus caroliniana | | American hornbram, ironwood | United States (Texas) |
| Carya cordiformis | | Bitternut hickory | United States (Texas) |
| Cersis canadensis | | Eastern redbud | United States |
| Chionanthus retusus | | Chinese fringe tree | China |
| Cornus florida | | Flowering dogwood | United States |
| Crataegus marshallii | | Parsley hawthorn | Southeastern United States |
| Crataegus opaca | | May hawthorn, mayhaw | Southeastern United States |
| Crataegus texana | | Texas hawthorn | United States (Texas) |
| Cyrtomium falcatum | | Holly fern | United States |
| Euonymus americana | | Strawberry bush | United States (Texas) |
| Ficus pumila | | Fig ivy | East Asia |
| Fraxinus pennsylvanica | | Green ash | United States |
| Gardenia jasminoides | 'Prostrata' | Dwarf gardenia, cape jasmine | China |
| Gardenia jasminoides | | Gardenia | China |
| Gardenia thunbergia | | Hip gardenia | South Africa |
| Ginkgo biloba | | Ginkgo, maidenhair tree | China |
| Gordonia lasianthus | | Loblolly bay | Southeastern United States |
| Halesia diptera | | Two-winged silverbell | Southern United States |
| Halesia diptera var. magnaflora | | Two-winged silverbell | Southern United States |
| Hamamelis virginiana | | Witch hazel | United States |

| Botanical Name | Hybrid/Cultivar | Common Name | Origin |
|---|---|---|---|
| *Hibiscus syriacus* | | Althaea, rose of Sharon | East Asia |
| *Hydrangea macrophylla* | | French hydrangea | Japan |
| *Hydrangea macrophylla* | 'Tricolor' | Variegated hydrangea | Japan, China |
| *Hydrangea quercifolia* | | Oak-leaf hydrangea | Southeastern United States |
| *Ilex opaca* | | American holly | United States |
| *Ilex opaca* | 'Savannah' | Savannah holly | United States |
| *Ilex vomitoria* | 'Lynn Lowrey' | Columnar yaupon holly | United States (Texas) |
| *Ilex vomitoria* | 'Nana' | Dwarf yaupon holly | United States (Texas) |
| *Ilex vomitoria* | | Yaupon holly | Southern United States |
| *Illicium floridanum* | | White Florida anise | Southern United States |
| *Iris cristata* | 'Nada' | Dwarf crested iris | United States |
| *Itea verginica* | | Virginia sweetspire | |
| *Lagerstromia indica* | 'Muskogee' | Crepe myrtle | China |
| *Lagerstromia indica* | 'Natchez' | Crepe myrtle | China |
| *Lagerstromia indica* | 'Near East' | Crepe myrtle | China |
| *Leucojum aestivum* | | Summer snowflake | Europe |
| *Ligularia tussilaginea* | | Ligularia | Japan, Korea |
| *Ligularia tussilaginea albo variegat* | | White-blotched ligularia | Japan, China |
| *Ligustrum* | | Privet | China |
| *Ligustrum japonicum* | | Wax-leaf ligustrum | China |
| *Liquidambar styraciflua* | | Sweet gum | United States (Texas) |
| *Liriodendron tulipifera* | | Tulip poplar | United States |
| *Liriope muscari* | | Giant liriope | China |
| *Liriope muscari* | 'Munroe Whiter' | White-blooming liriope | Japan, China |
| *Lobularia maritima* | | Sweet alyssum | Europe |
| *Lonciera fragrantissima* | | Bush honeysuckle | China |
| *Loropetalum chinense* | 'Alba' | Chinese witch hazel | Japan, China |
| *Magnolia denudata* | | Yulan magnolia | China |
| *Magnolia grandiflora* | | Southern magnolia | Southern United States |
| *Magnolia macrophylla* | | Bigleaf magnolia | United States |
| *Magnolia sieboldii* | | Oyama magnolia | Japan, Korea |
| *Magnolia stellata* | 'Dr. Merrill' | Star magnolia | Japan |
| *Magnolia stellata* | | Star magnolia | Japan |
| *Magnolia virginiana* | | Sweetbay magnolia | United States (Texas) |
| *Magnolia x soulangiana* | 'Full Eclipse' | Saucer magnolia | China |
| *Magnolia x soulangiana* | 'Jon Jon' | Saucer magnolia | China |
| *Magnolia x soulangiana* | 'Pink Goblet' | Saucer magnolia | China |
| *Magnolia x soulangiana* | 'Todd Gresham' | Saucer magnolia | China |
| *Magnolia x soulangiana* | | Saucer magnolia | China |
| *Malphia glabra* | | Dwarf Barbados cherry | South America |
| *Malus purpurea* | 'Eleyi' | Flowering crab apple | China |
| *Michelia figo* | | Banana shrub | China |
| *Michelia x foggii* | | Banana shrub | China |

| Botanical Name | Hybrid/Cultivar | Common Name | Origin |
| --- | --- | --- | --- |
| Microlepia strigosa | | Asian fern | Asia, Polynesia |
| Nyssa aquatica | | Water tupelo | |
| Ophiopogon japonicus | 'Variegatus' | Aztec grass | Japan, China |
| Ophiopogon japonicus | 'Nana' | Dwarf mondo grass | Japan, Korea |
| Ophiopogon japonicus | | Mondo grass | Japan, China |
| Osmanthus fragrans | | Sweet olive | East Asia |
| Osmanthus heterophyllus | | False holly | China |
| Osmunda cinnamomea | | Cinnamon fern | United States |
| Osmunda regalis | | Royal fern | Africa |
| Ostrya virginiana | | American hop hornbeam | United States |
| Oxalis regnallii | | White clover | South America |
| Pentas lanceolata | | Penta | Tropical Africa |
| Philadelphus coronarius | | Mock orange | Southeast Asia |
| Pinius taeda | | Loblolly pine | United States |
| Pistacia texana | | Texas pistache | United States (Texas) |
| Platanus occidentalis | | American sycamore | United States |
| Podocarpus Macrophyllus | | Japanese yew | Japan |
| Polypodium scouleri | | Leather-leaf fern | United States |
| Polystichium acxastichaides | | Christmas fern | United States |
| Prunus caroliniana | | Cherry laurel | United States (Texas) |
| Prunus mexicana | | Mexican plum | Mexico |
| Quercus alba | | White oak | United States |
| Quercus falcata var. leucophylla | | Cherry-bark red oak | United States (Texas) |
| Quercus falcata var. pagodifolia | | Swamp red oak | United States (Texas) |
| Quercus lyrata | | Overcup oak | United States (Texas) |
| Quercus nigra | | Water oak | United States |
| Quercus polymorpha | | Monterrey oak | Mexico |
| Quercus prinus | | Swamp chestnut oak | Southeastern United States |
| Quercus shumardii | | Shumard's red oak | United States |
| Quercus sinuata | | Durand oak | United States (Texas) |
| Rhododendron indicum | 'Salmon Solomon' | Azalea—Belgian hybrid | Japan |
| Rhododendron indicum | 'Christmas Cheer' | Azalea—Kurume hybrid | Japan |
| Rhododendron indicum | 'Coral Bells' | Azalea—Kurume hybrid | Japan |
| Rhododendron indicum | 'Hinode Giri' | Azalea—Kurume hybrid | Japan |
| Rhododendron indicum | 'Pink Pearl' | Azalea—Kurume hybrid | Japan |
| Rhododendron indicum | 'Madame Pericat' | Azalea—Pericat hybrid | Japan |
| Rhododendron indicum | 'Sweetheart 'Supreme' | Azalea—Pericat hybrid | Japan |
| Rhododendron indicum | 'Louise J. Bobbink' | Azalea—Rutherford hybrid | Japan |
| Rhododendron indicum | 'Pink Ruffles' | Azalea—Rutherford hybrid | Japan |
| Rhododendron indicum | 'Hexe' | Azalea—Sander and Foster hybrid | Japan |
| Rhododendron indicum | 'Fancy Gumpo' | Azalea—Satsuki hybrid | Japan |
| Rhododendron indicum | 'Pink Gumpo' | Azalea—Satsuki hybrid | Japan |
| Rhododendron indicum | 'Wakaebisu' | Azalea—Satsuki hybrid | Japan |

| Botanical Name | Hybrid/Cultivar | Common Name | Origin |
| --- | --- | --- | --- |
| Rhododendron indicum | 'Daphne Salmon' | Azalea—Southern Indica hybrid | Japan |
| Rhododendron indicum | 'Elegans' | Azalea—Southern Indica hybrid | Japan |
| Rhododendron indicum | 'Fielder's White' | Azalea—Southern Indica hybrid | Japan |
| Rhododendron indicum | 'Fisher Pink' | Azalea—Southern Indica hybrid | Japan |
| Rhododendron indicum | 'Formosa' | Azalea—Southern Indica hybrid | Japan |
| Rhododendron indicum | 'George Lindsey Tabor' | Azalea—Southern Indica hybrid | Japan |
| Rhododendron indicum | 'Gulf Pride' | Azalea—Southern Indica hybrid | Japan |
| Rhododendron indicum | 'Judge Solmon' | Azalea—Southern Indica hybrid | Japan |
| Rhododendron indicum | 'Kate Arendall' | Azalea—Southern Indica hybrid | Japan |
| Rhododendron indicum | 'Mardi Gras' | Azalea—Southern Indica hybrid | Japan |
| Rhododendron indicum | 'Mrs. G. G. Gerbing' | Azalea—Southern Indica hybrid | Japan |
| Rhododendron indicum | 'Pride of Mobile' | Azalea—Southern Indica hybrid | Japan |
| Rosa laevigata | | Cherokee rose | China |
| Rosa x rehderana | 'Ducher' | Antique rose (polyantha) | China |
| Rosa x rehderana | 'Marie Pavie' | Antique rose (polyantha) | China |
| Rosa x rehderana | 'The Fairy' | Antique rose (polyantha) | China |
| Sassafras albidum | | Sassafras | United States (Texas) |
| Saxifraga stolonifera | | Strawberry geranium | Eastern Asia |
| Sinjackia rehderana | | Jack tree, sinojakia | China |
| Sophora secundifolia | | Texas mountain laurel | United States (Texas) |
| Spiraea cantoniensis | | Reeve's spirea | China |
| Spiraea x vanhouttei | | Bridal wreath spirea | Garden |
| Thelypteris kunthii | | Wood fern | United States |
| Tilia americana | | Basswood, American linden | United States (Texas) |
| Trachelospernum asiaticum | | Asian jasmine | Japan, Korea |
| Ugnandia speciosa | | Mexican buckeye | Mexico, United States (Texas) |
| Ulmus alata | | Winged elm | United States (Texas) |
| Ulmus americana | | American elm | United States |
| Ulmus crassifolia | | Cedar elm | United States (Texas) |
| Ulmus parvifolia | 'Drake' | Drake elm | China |
| Verbena x hybida | 'Apple Blossom' | Verbena | Garden |
| Viburnum dentatum | | Arrowwood viburnum | United States (Texas) |
| Viburnum macrocephalum | | Chinese snowball viburnum | China |
| Viola odorata | | Sweet violet | Europe |
| Viola tricolor x wittrockiana | 'Happy Face' | Pansy | Garden |
| Viola tricolor x wittrockiana | 'Lake of Thun' | Pansy | Garden |
| Viola tricolor x wittrockiana | 'Steel Swiss Blue' | Pansy | Garden |
| Wisteria floribunda | | Japanese wisteria | Japan |
| Woodsia abtusa | | Blue laded woodsia fern | Europe |
| Xylosma congestum | | Xylosma | China |
| Zephyranthes candida | | Rain lily | South America |

# BIBLIOGRAPHY

Allegrezza, Kelly McCaughey. "Ruth London (1893–1966): Houston Landscape Architect." Master's thesis, Louisiana State University, 1999.

Banttari, Sally Robert. "The Evolution of the Bayou Bend Gardens, Houston, Texas (1926–1989)." Master's thesis, Louisiana State University, 1989.

Barnstone, Howard. *The Architecture of John F. Staub: Houston and the South.* Austin: University of Texas Press, 1979.

Bayou Bend Collection and Gardens Records. The Museum of Fine Arts, Houston, Archives.

Birnbaum, Charles A., and Robin Karson, eds. *Pioneers of American Landscape Design.* New York: McGraw Hill, 2000.

Cothran, James R. *Gardens and Historical Plants of the Antebellum South.* Columbia, South Carolina: University of South Carolina Press, 2003.

Cotner, Robert C. *James Stephen Hogg, A Biography.* Austin: University of Texas Press, 1959.

Ferguson, Cheryl Caldwell. "River Oaks: 1920s Suburban Planning and Development in Houston." *Southwestern Historical Quarterly* (Texas State Historical Association) 104, no. 2 (October 2000).

Forum of Civics. *A Garden Book for Houston.* Houston: privately printed for the Forum of Civics, 1929.

Garden Club of America. *Gardens of America.* Privately printed by the Garden Club of America, 1935.

Griswold, Mac, and Eleanor Weller. *The Golden Age of American Gardens: Proud Owners, Private Estates, 1890–1930.* New York: Harry N. Abrams, 1991.

Hogg, Ima, Papers and William C. Hogg Papers. Center for American History. The University of Texas at Austin.

Hood, David F. "The Renaissance of Southern Gardens in the Early Twentieth Century." *Journal of Garden History* 16, no. 2 (April–June 1996).

Houghton, Dorothy Knox Howe, Barrie Scardino, Sadie Gwin Blackburn, and Katherine S. Howe. *Houston's Forgotten Heritage: Landscape, Houses, Interiors, 1824–1914.* Houston: Rice University Press, 1991.

Hume, H. Harold. *Azaleas and Camellias.* New York: Macmillan, 1931.

Johnston, Marguerite. *Houston, The Unknown City, 1836–1946.* College Station, Texas: Texas A&M University Press, 1991.

King, Louisa Yeomans (Mrs. Francis). *Variety in the Little Garden.* Boston: The Atlantic Monthly Press, 1923.

Lomax, John. *Will Hogg, Texan.* Austin: University of Texas Press, 1956.

Neff, Emily Ballew. *Frederic Remington: The Hogg Brothers Collection of the Museum of Fine Arts, Houston.* Princeton: Princeton University Press, 2000.

Staub, John F. "Latin Colonial Architecture." *Southern Architect and Building News* (August 1930).

———. "Latin Colonial Architecture in the Southwest." *Civics for Houston* 1, no. 2 (February 1928).

Tankard, Judith. *The Gardens of Ellen Biddle Shipman.* Sagaponack, New York: Sagapress, Inc., 1996.

Warren, David B. "Bayou Bend: The Plan and History of the Gardens." *The Museum of Fine Arts, Houston, Bulletin* 12, no. 2 (winter-spring 1989).

Warren, David B., Michael K. Brown, Elizabeth Ann Coleman, and Emily Ballew Neff. *American Decorative Arts and Paintings in the Bayou Bend Collection.* Princeton: Princeton University Press, 1998.

# INDEX

## SEEDS

| | Date Ordered | FROM WHOM | No. of Packets | Date Received | Date and Place Planted | Date of Blooming |
|---|---|---|---|---|---|---|
| a | May '30 | Germain's | | | | |

## PLANTS & Bulbs

| TY | Date Ordered | FROM WHOM | No. of Plants | Date Received | Date and Place Planted | D Blo |
|---|---|---|---|---|---|---|
| bena | May '30 | Germain's (beautiful plants) | 2 | May | Lower garden "Upper garden" | |
| ium | May | Jos. W. Vestal | 2 | May | along wall | |
| ies | | Marshall | 100 | | Nov. 14 upper garden | |
| llow | | Marshall | 100 each | | Nov. 14 upper garden | |
| lies } lies } | } | Max Schling | 12 24 | | nov. 7 upper garden outer row | |